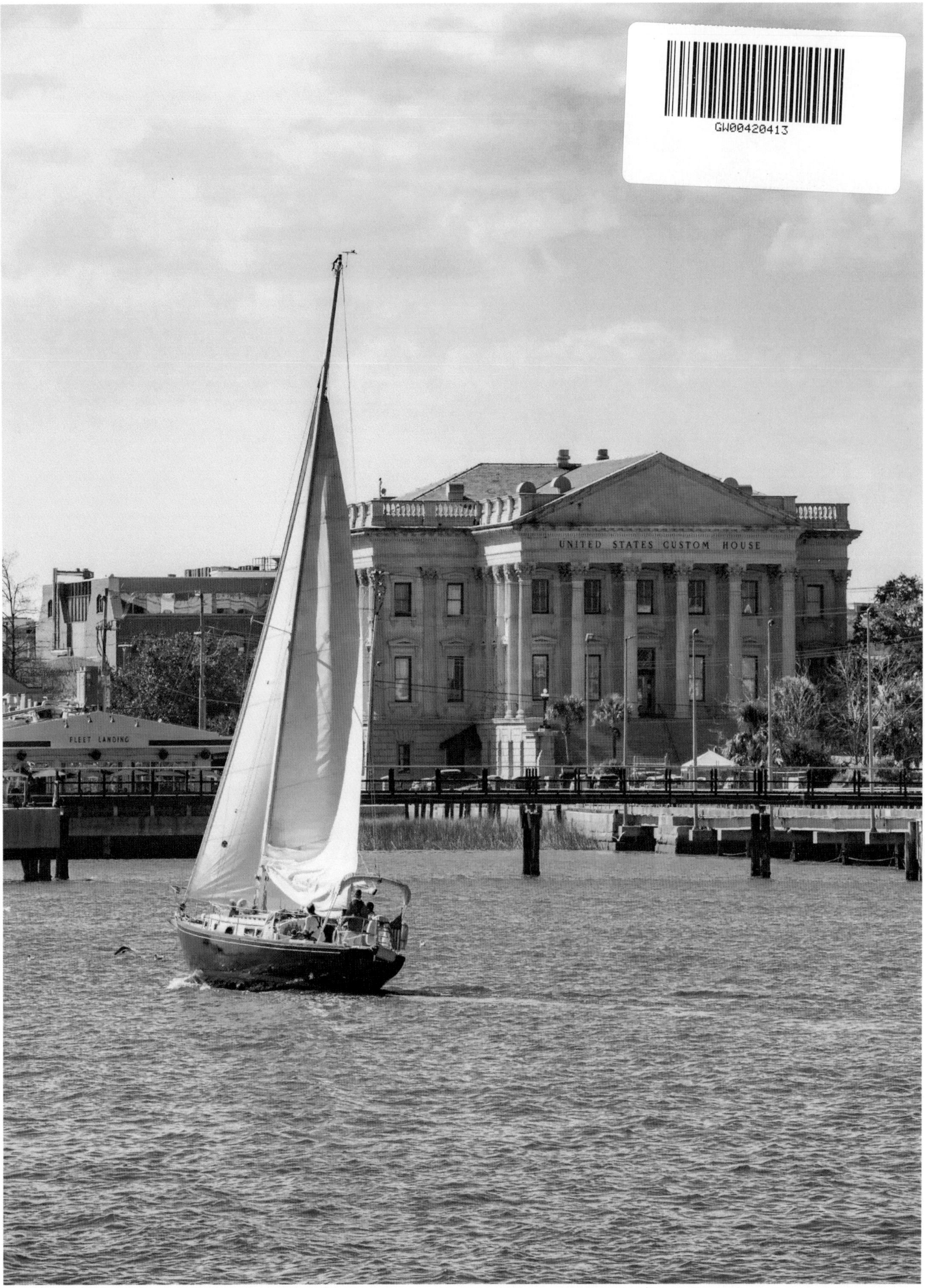
UNITED STATES CUSTOM HOUSE
FLEET LANDING

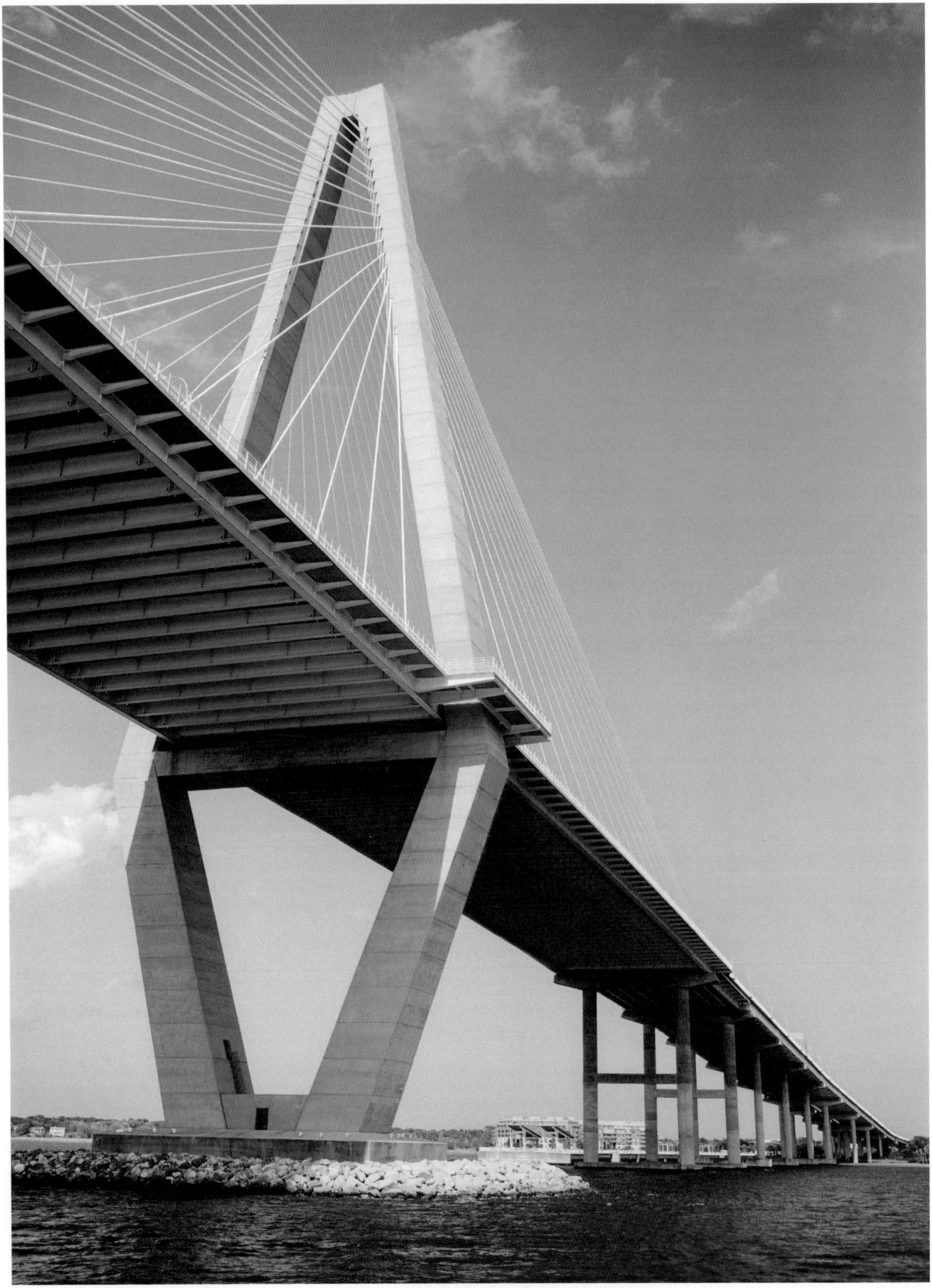

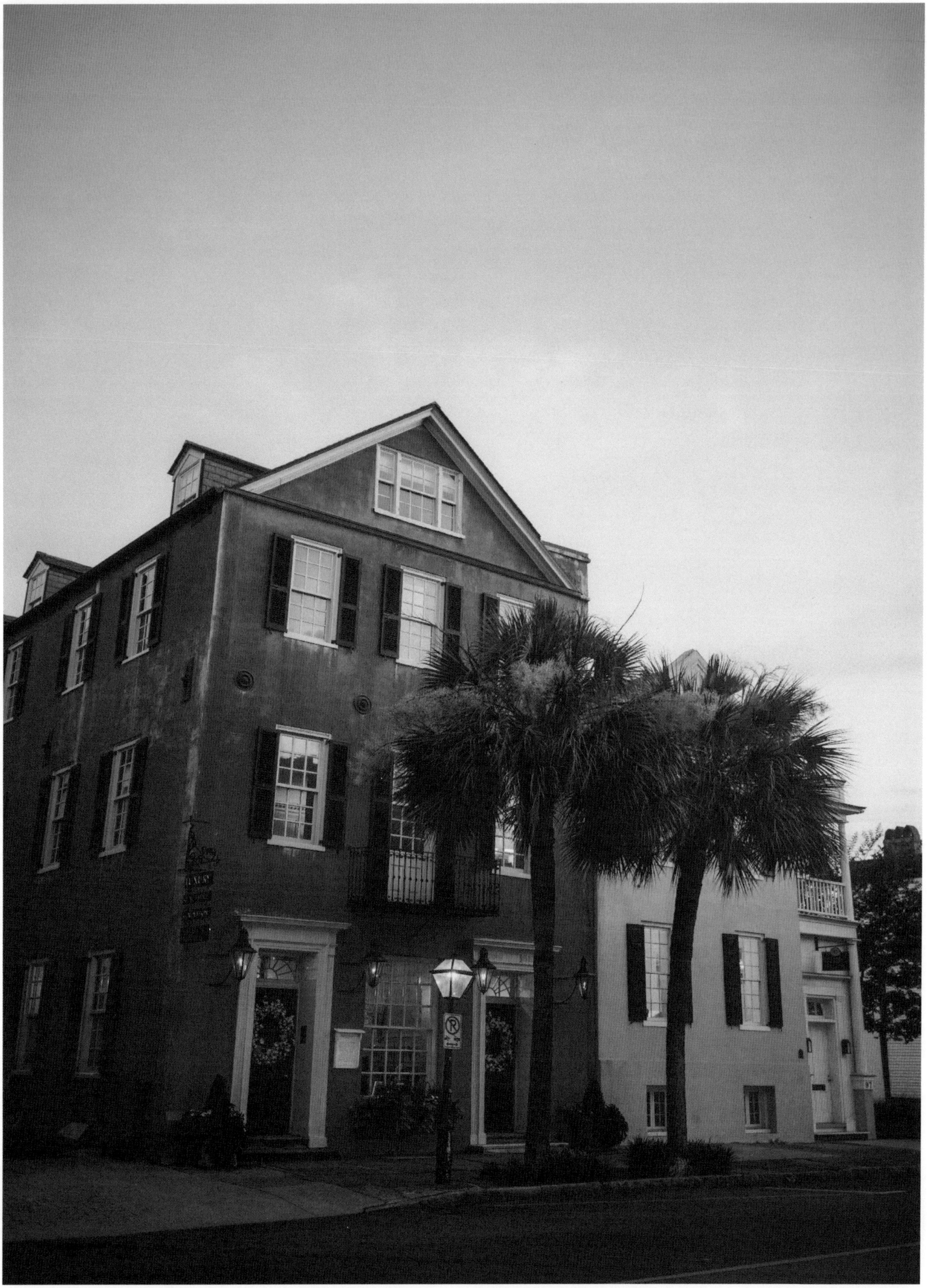

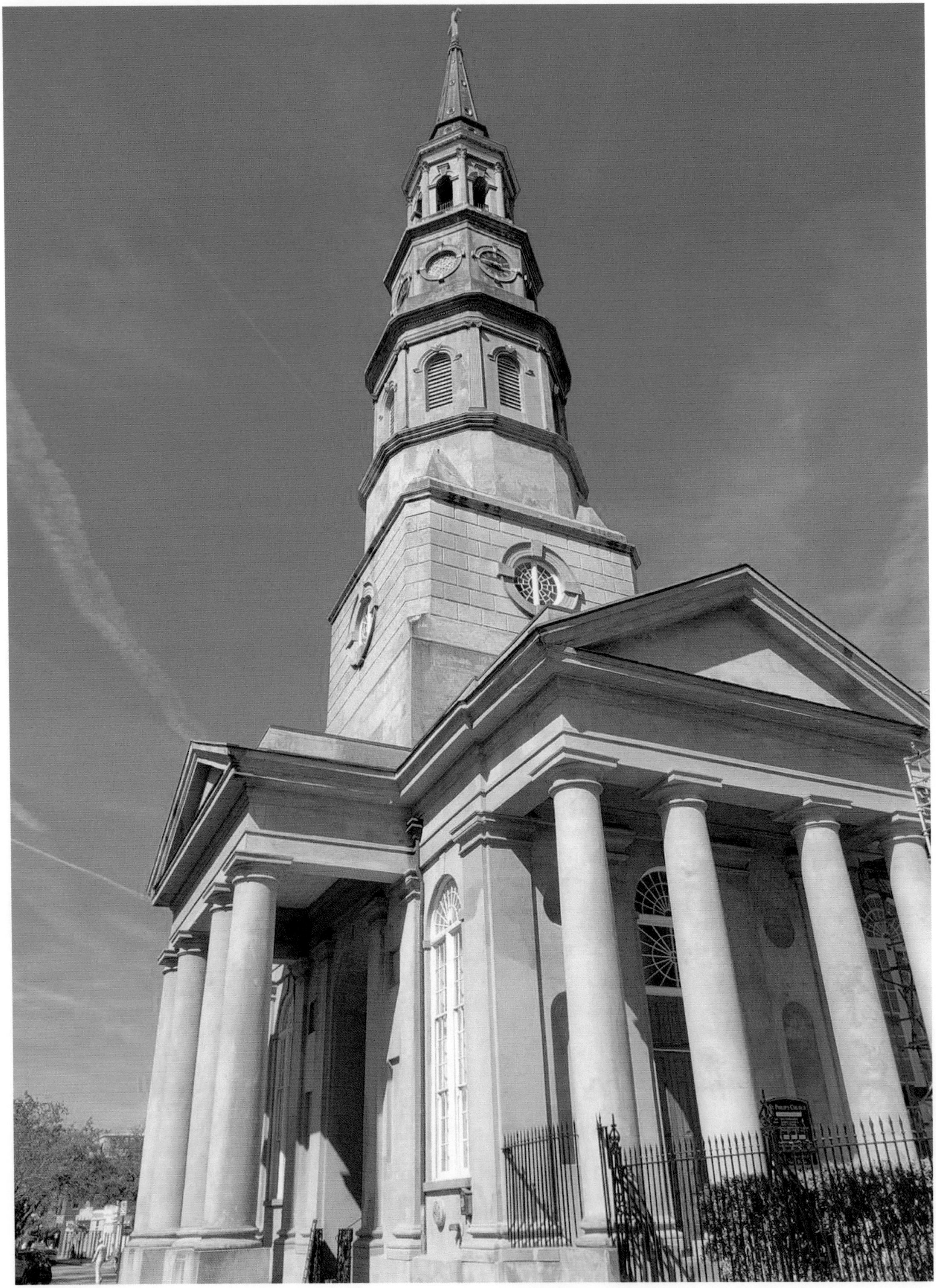

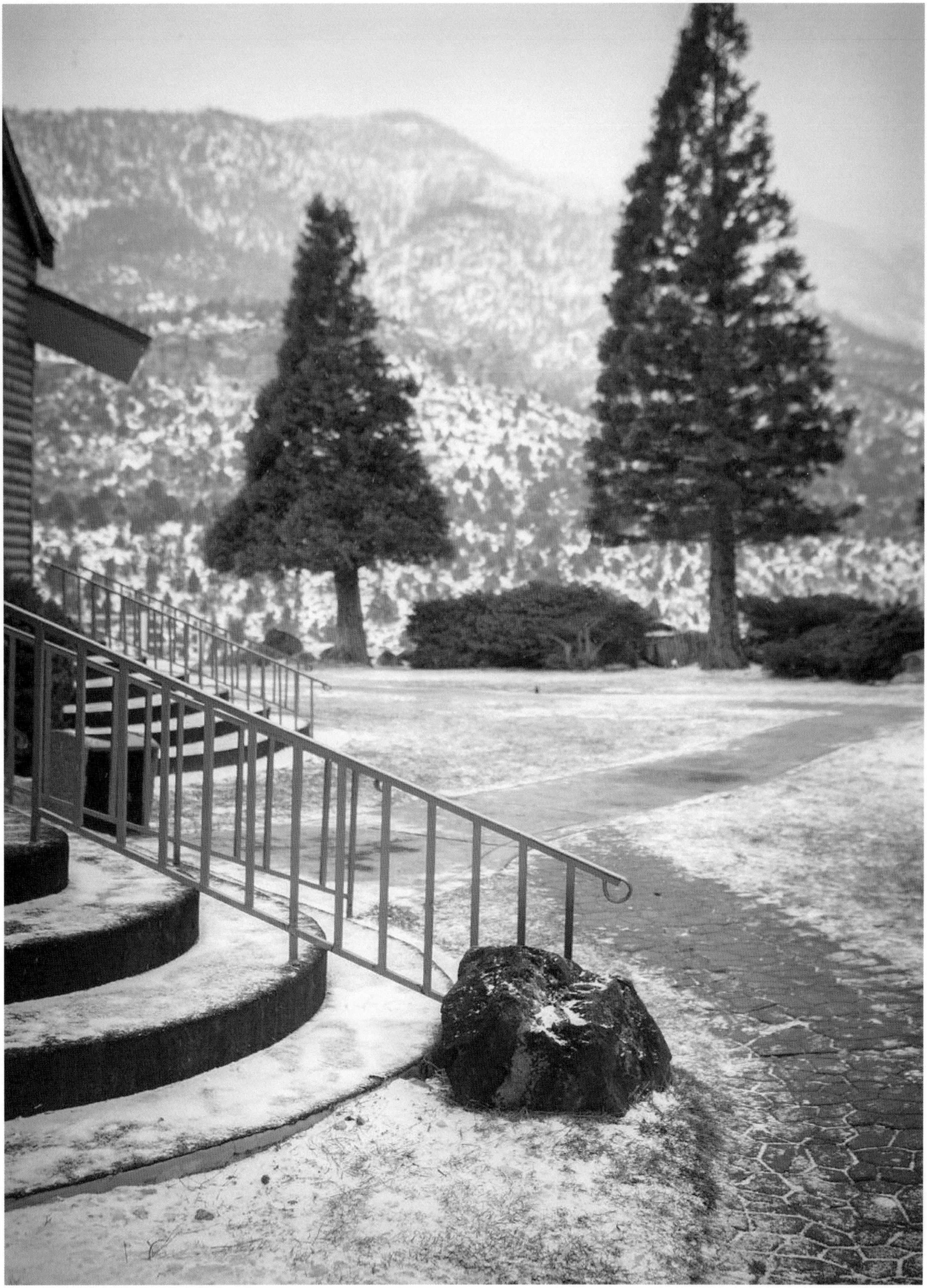

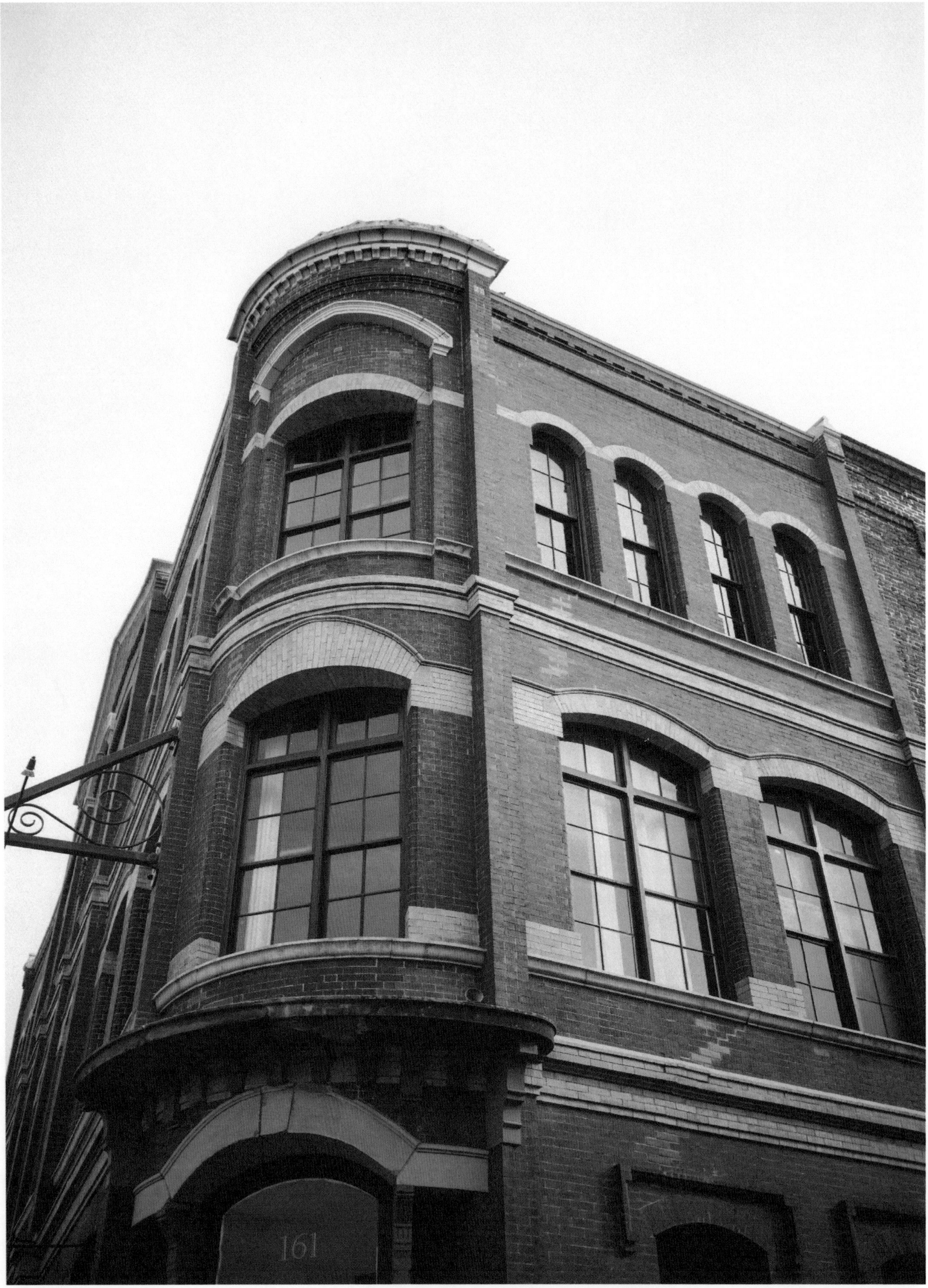
161

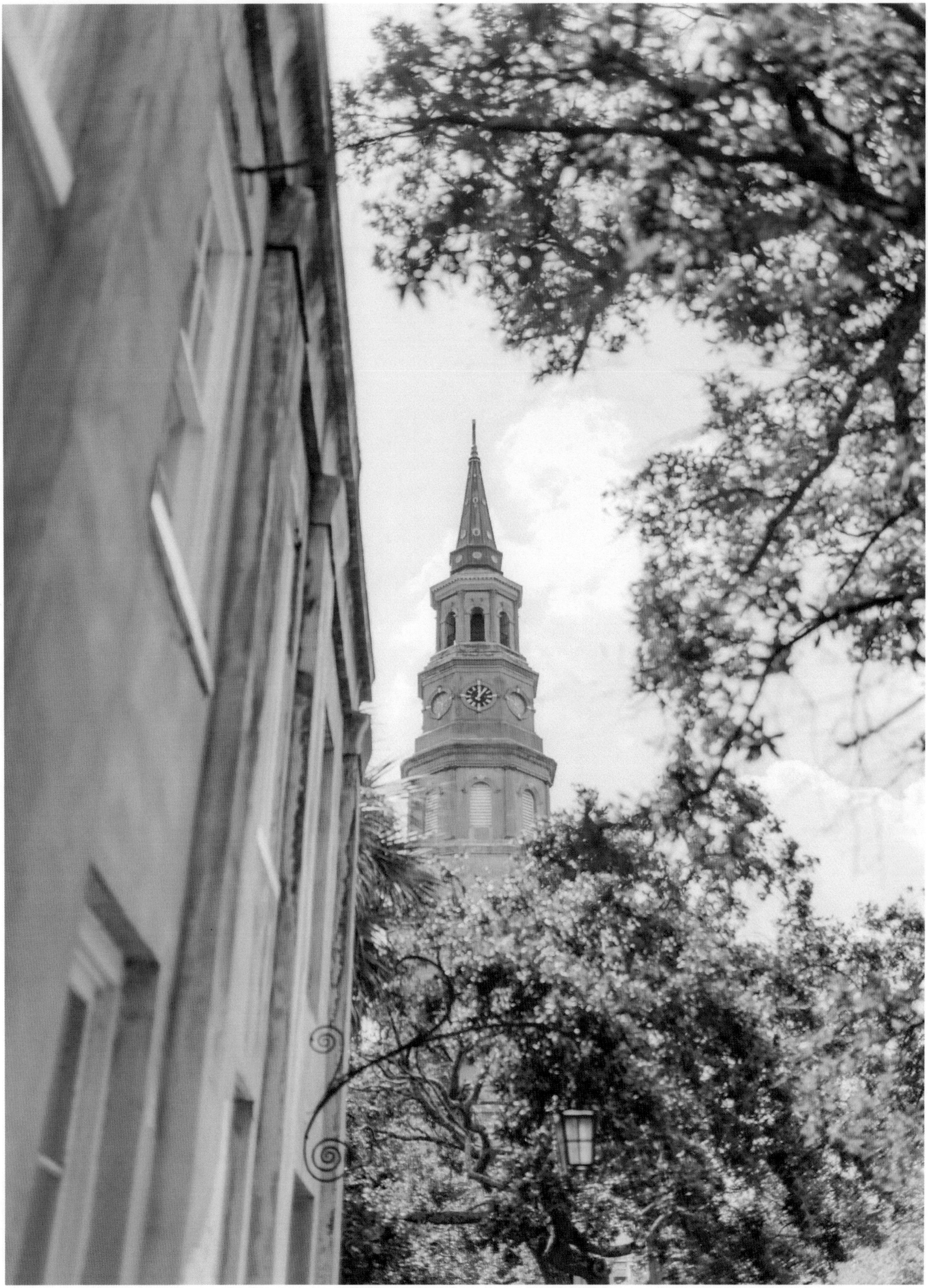

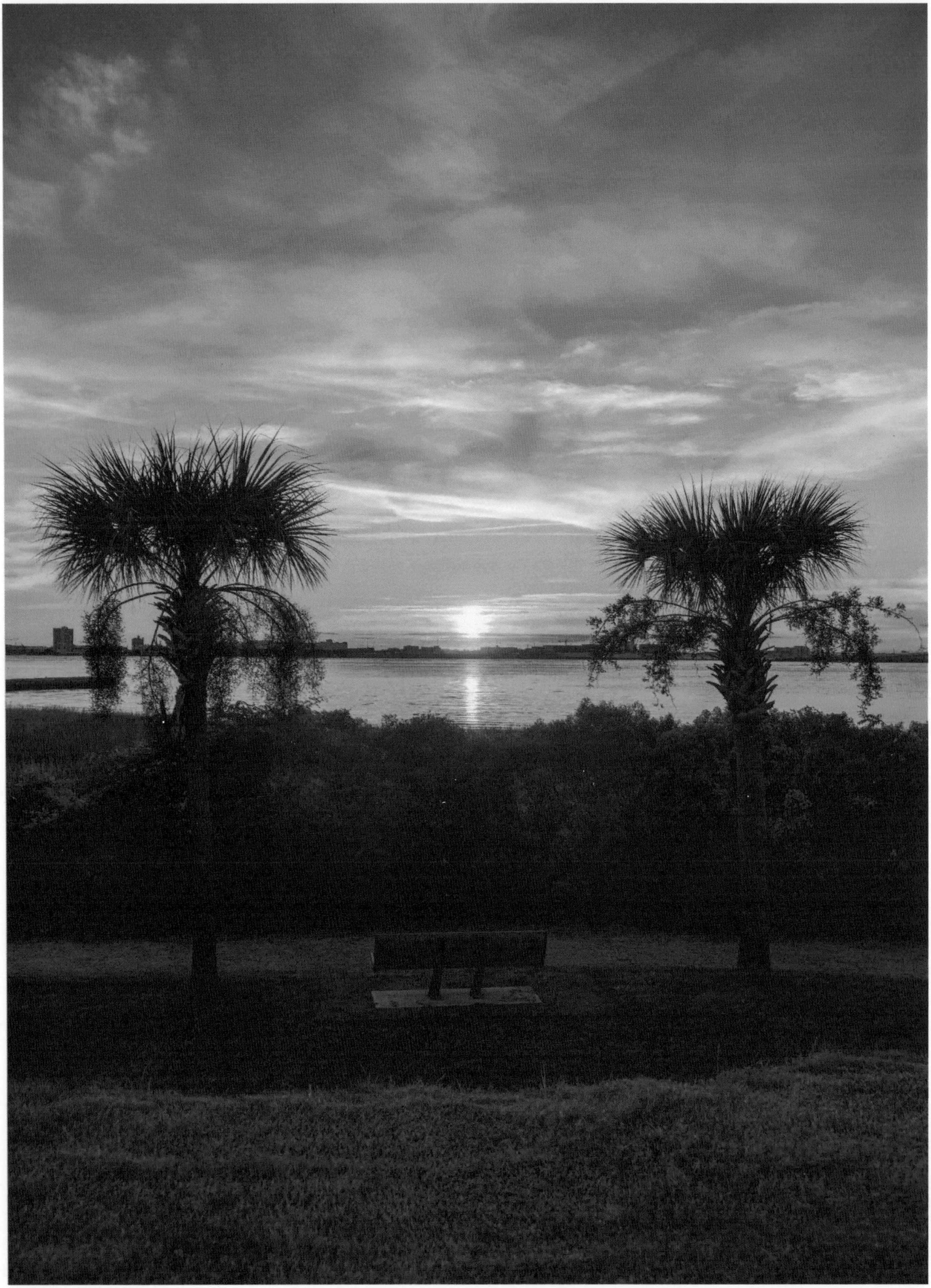

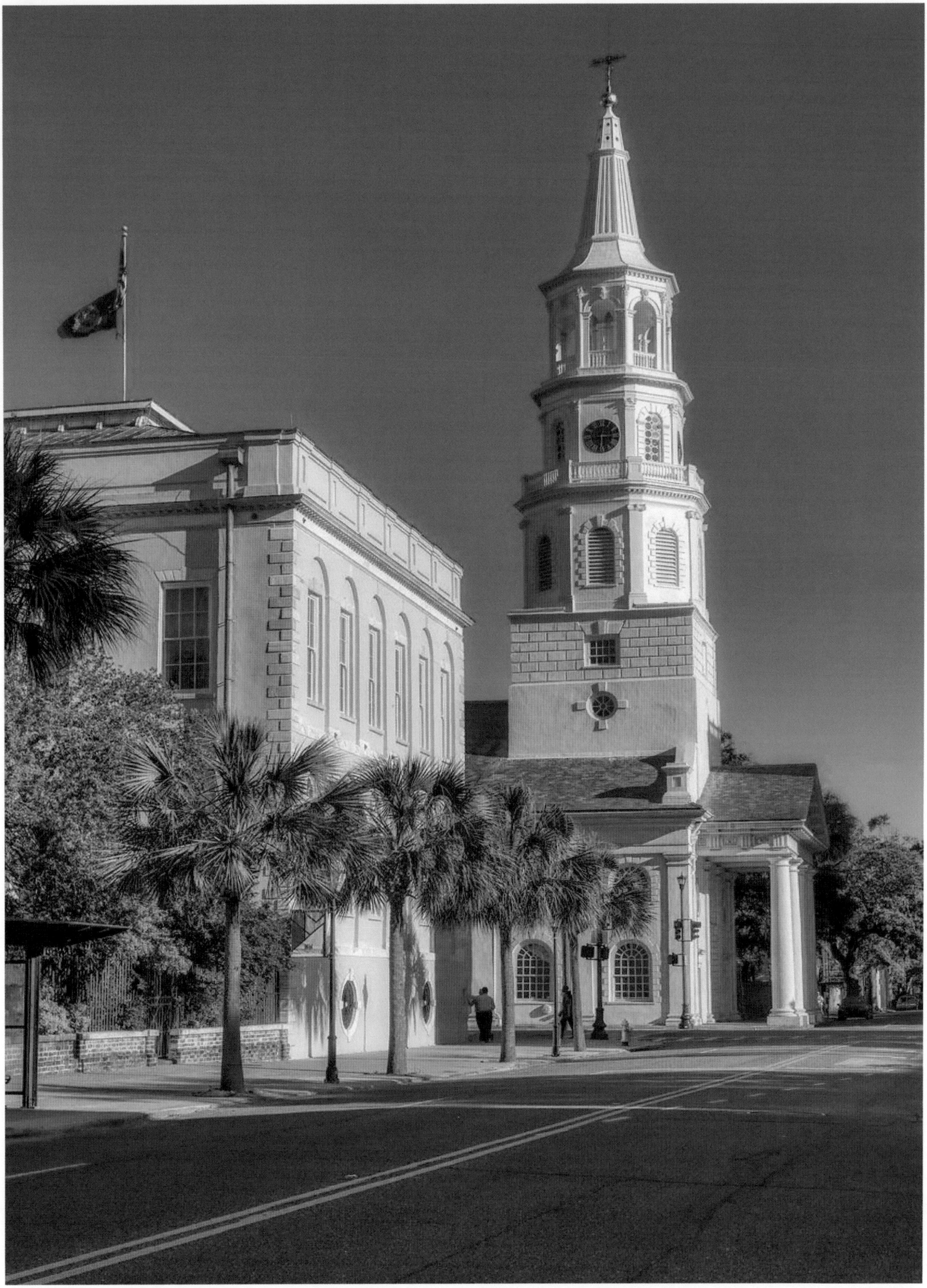

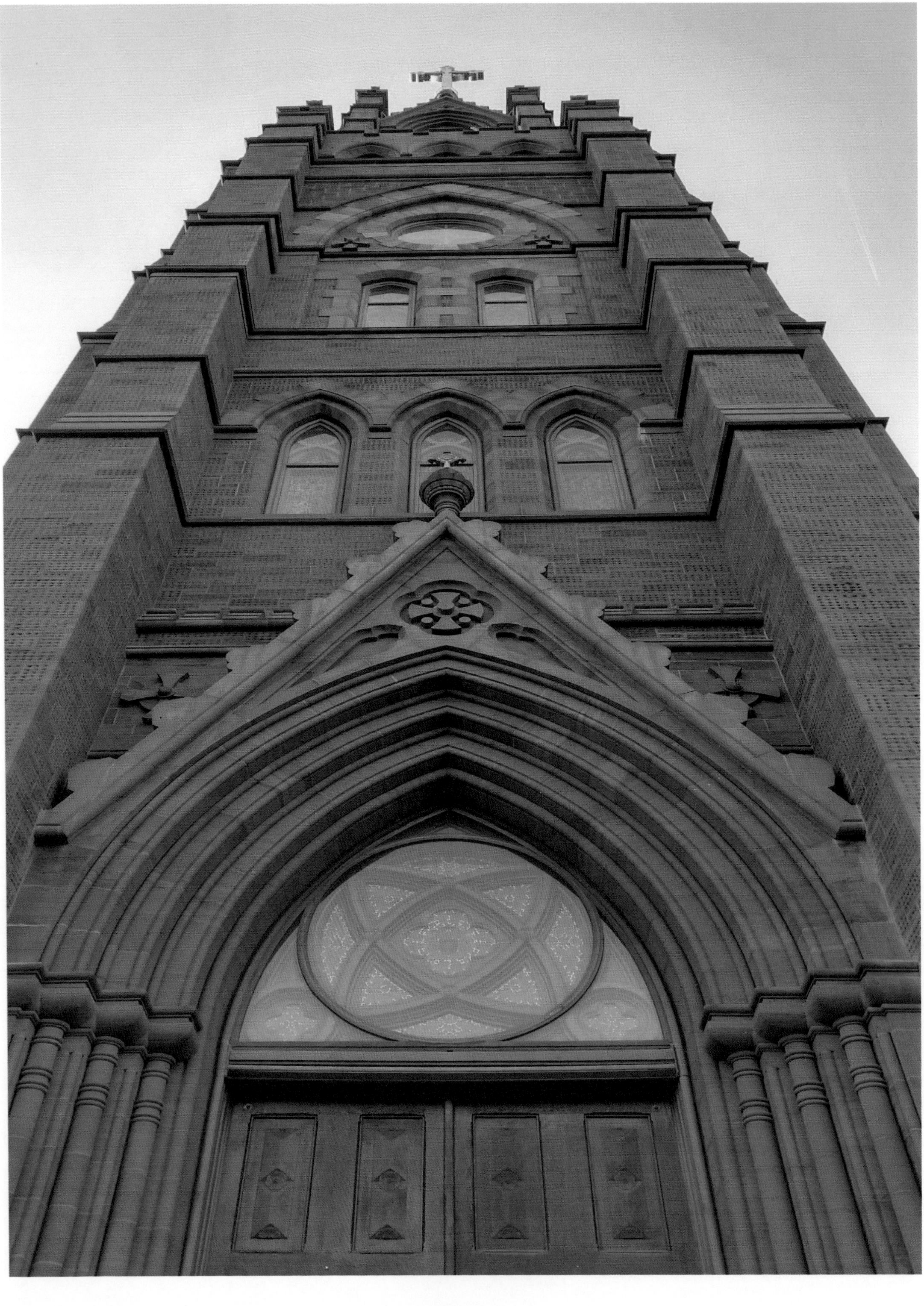

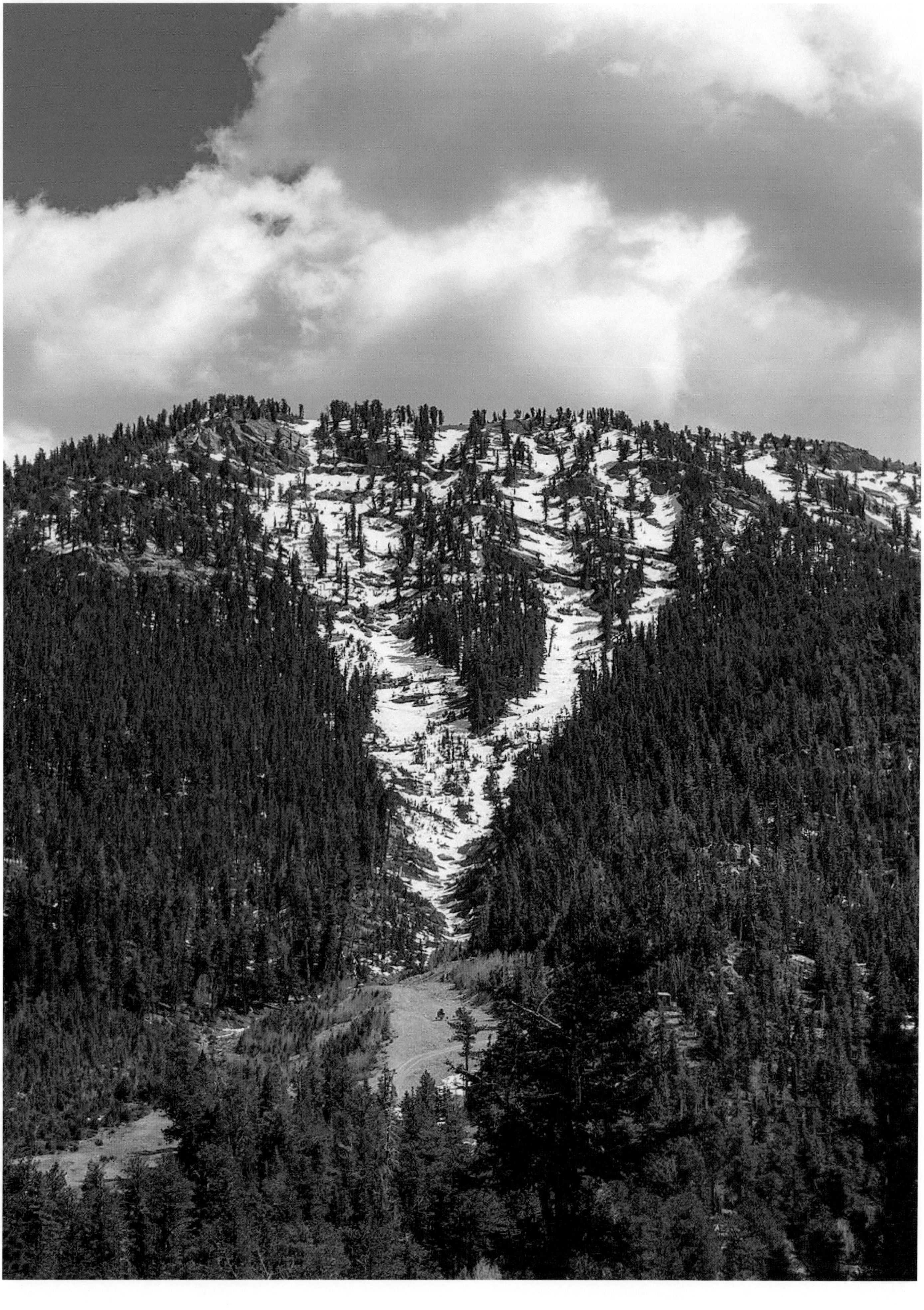

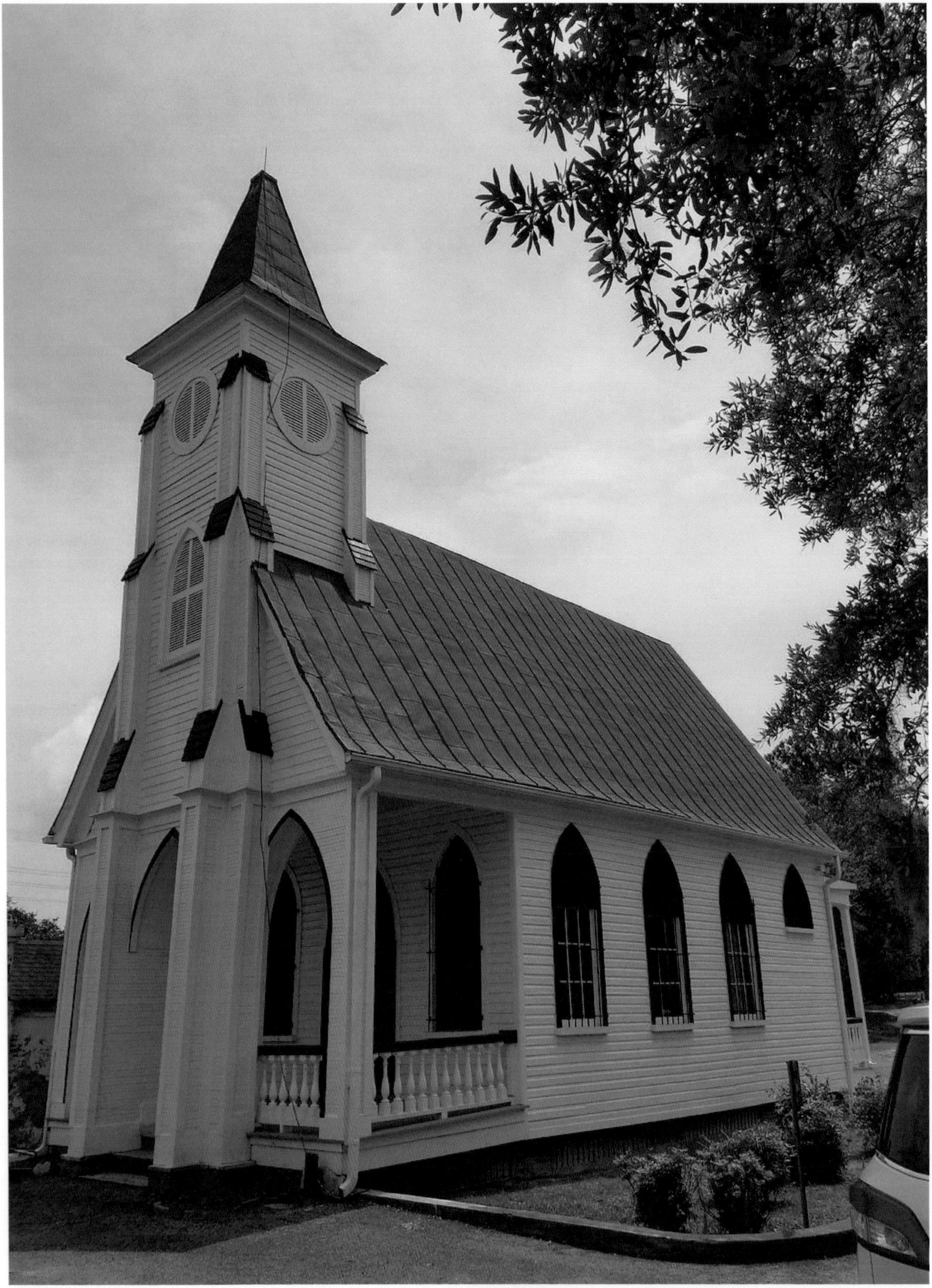

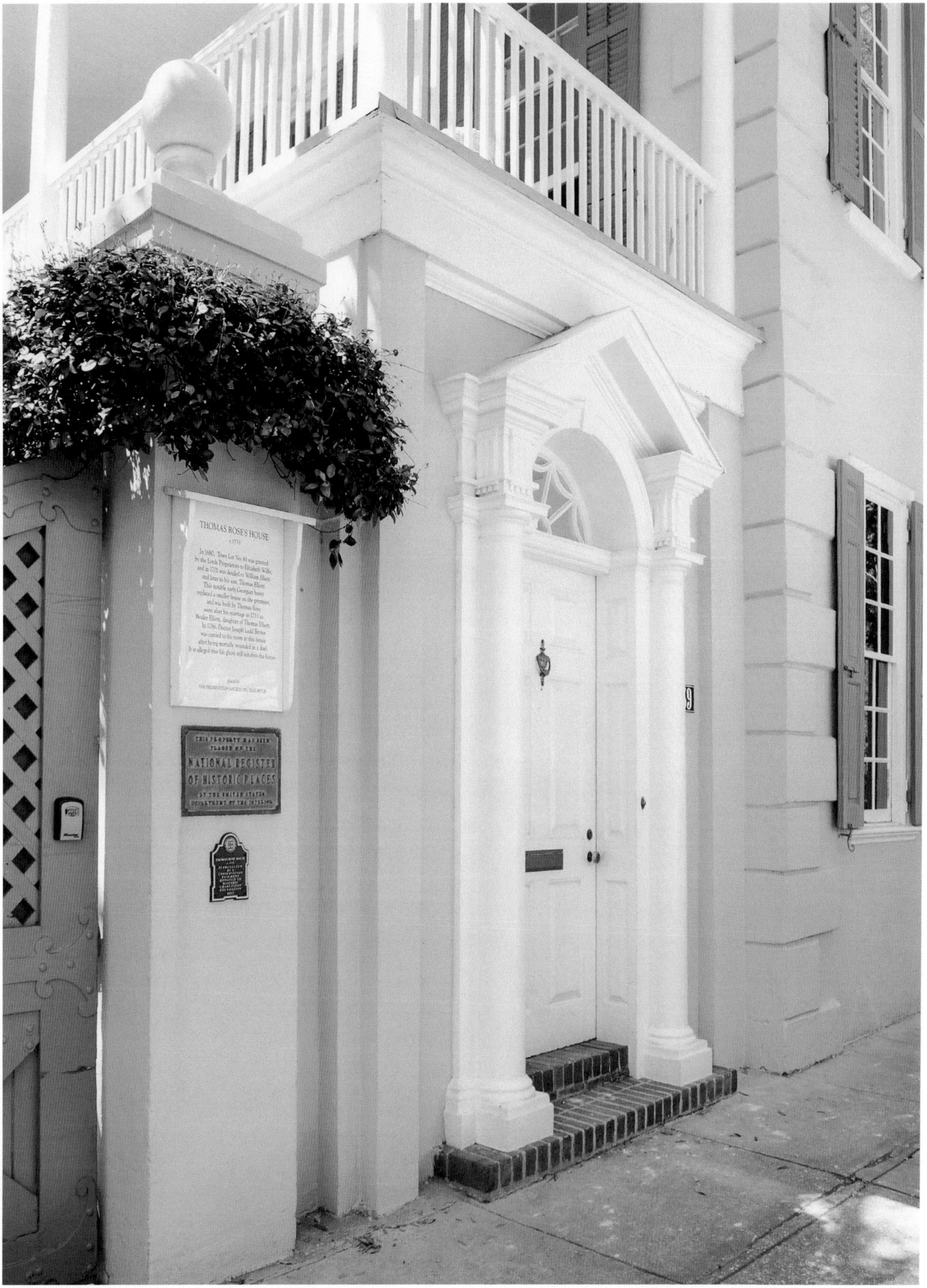
THOMAS ROSE'S HOUSE
NATIONAL REGISTER
OF HISTORIC PLACES
9

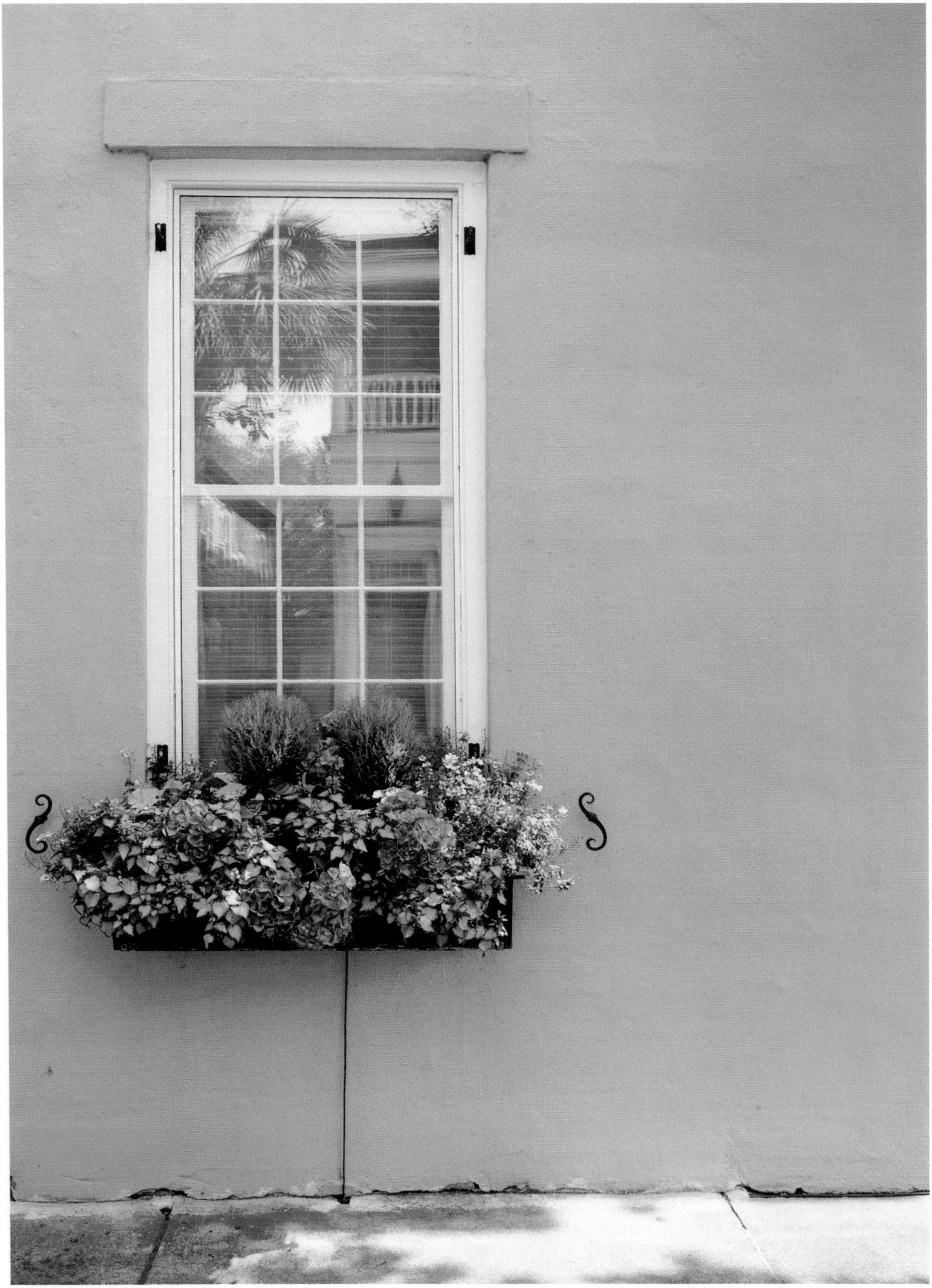

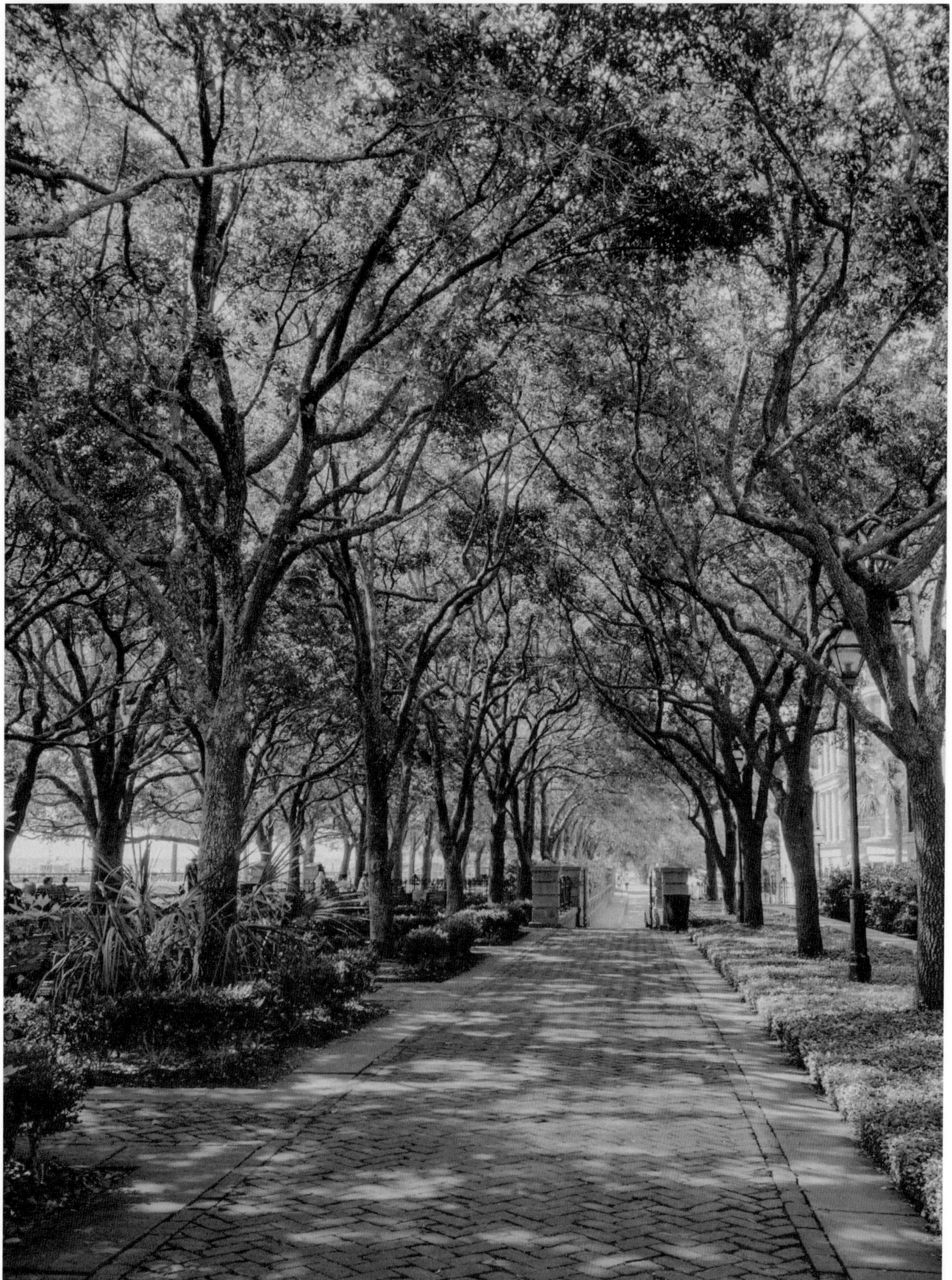

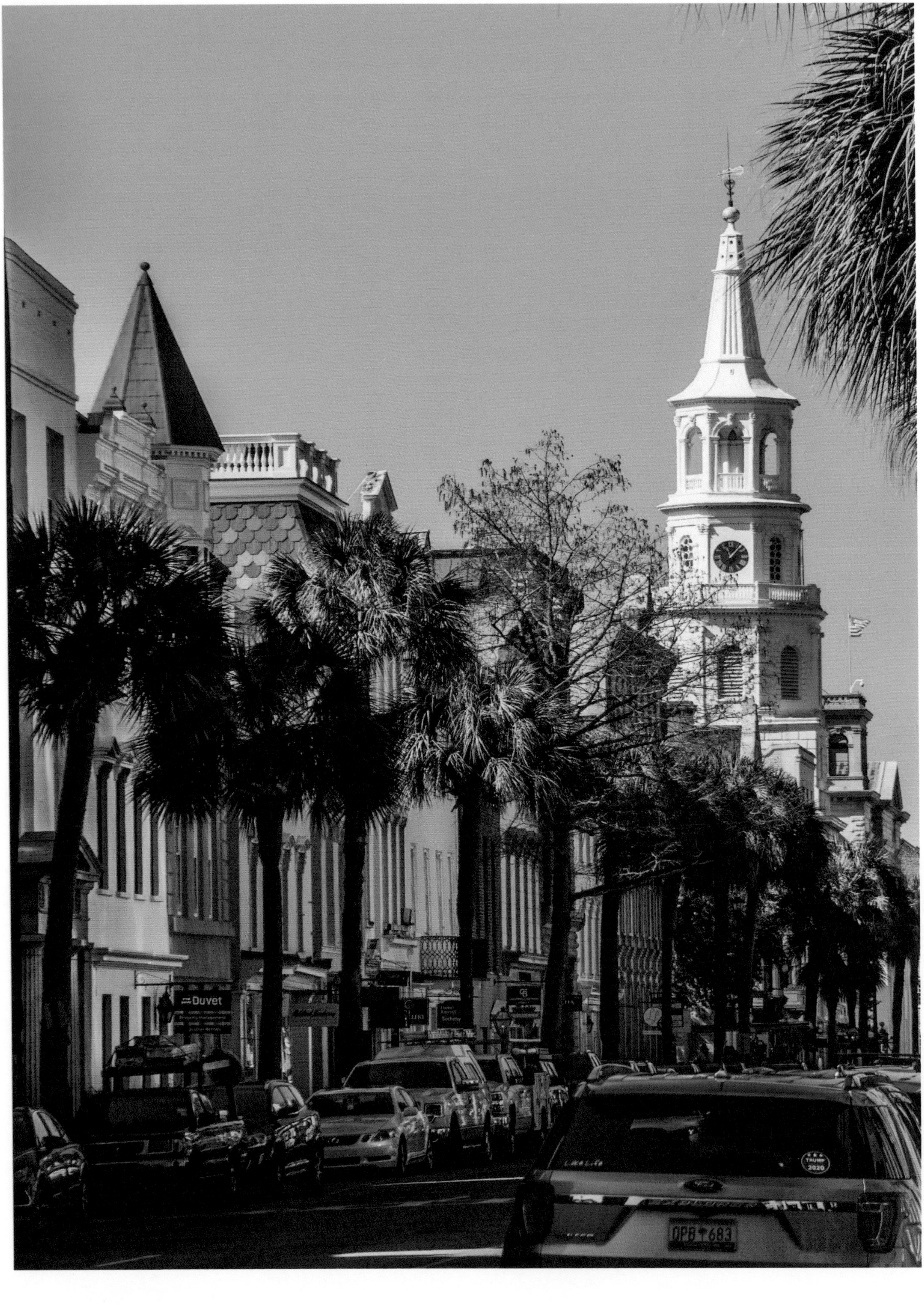
Duvet
TRUMP
2020

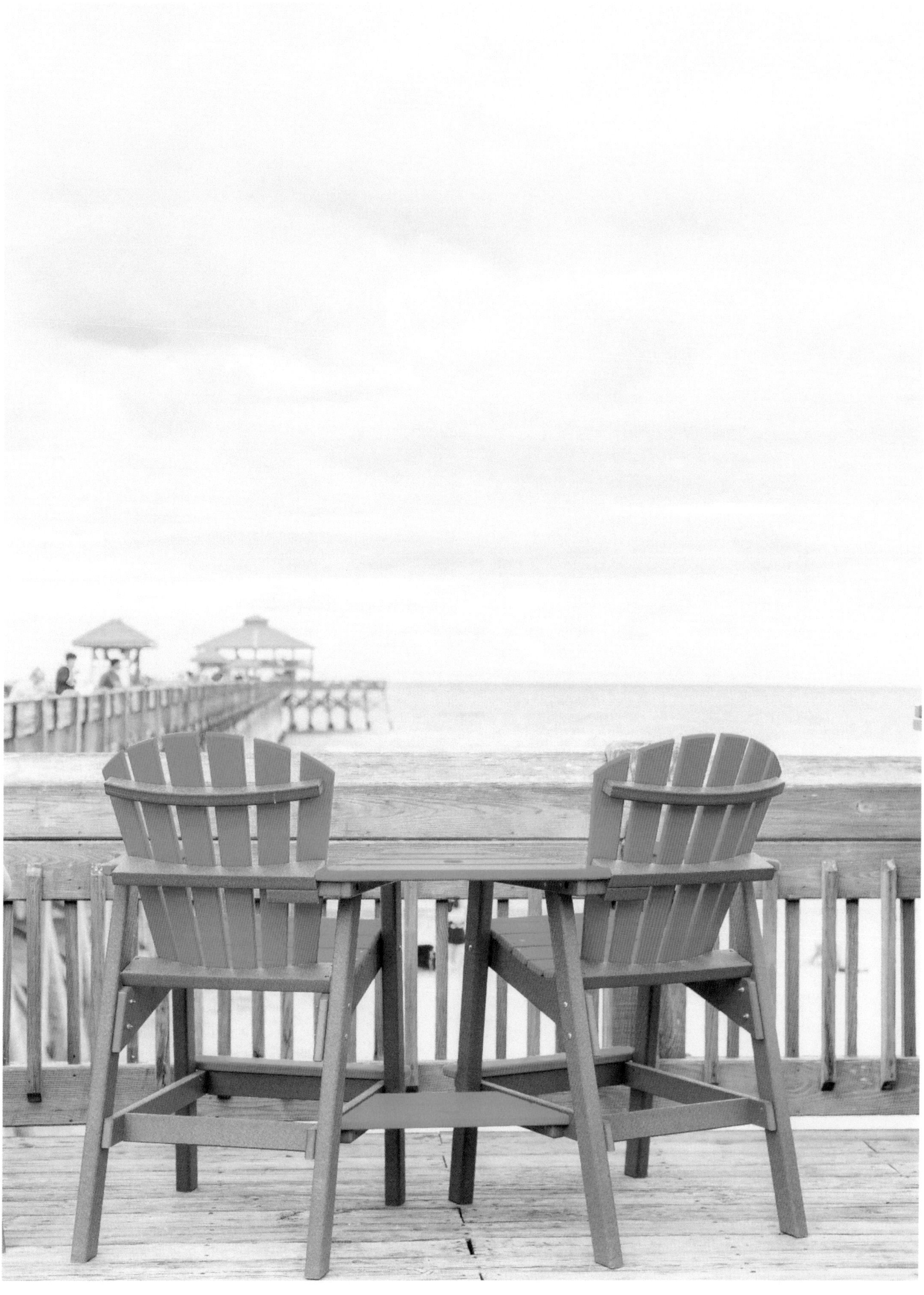

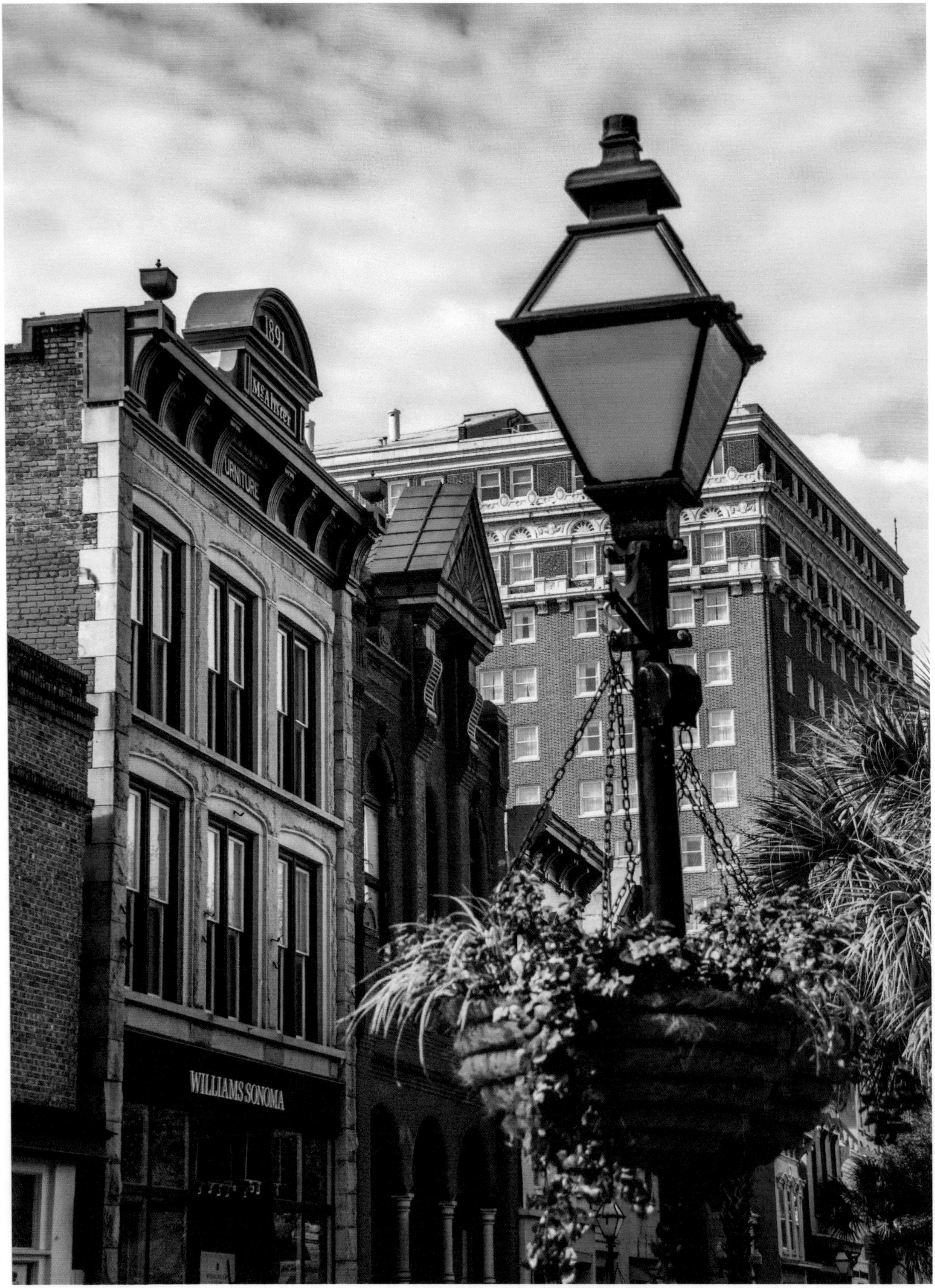
1891
McAlister
URNITURE
WILLIAMS SONOMA

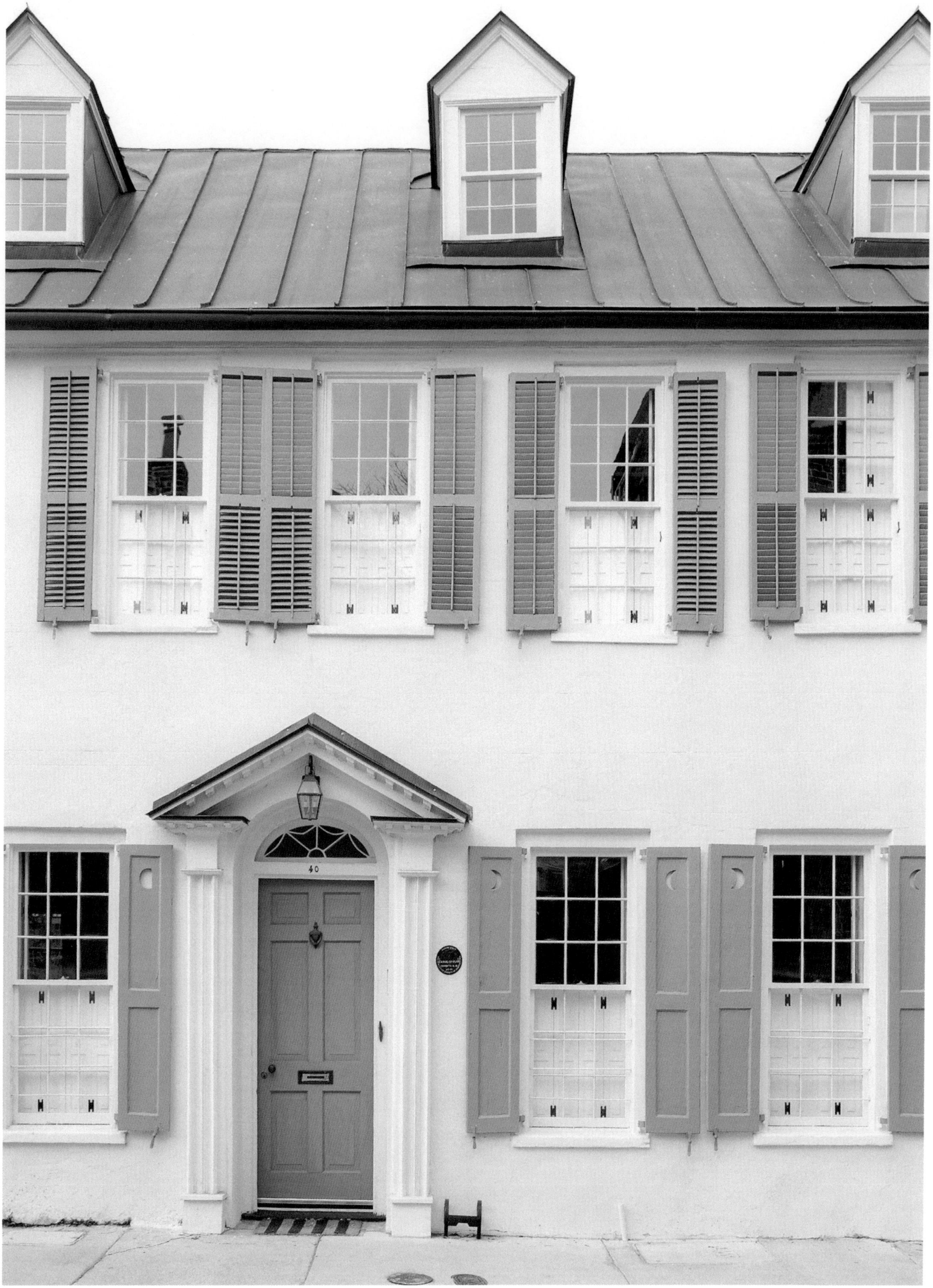
40

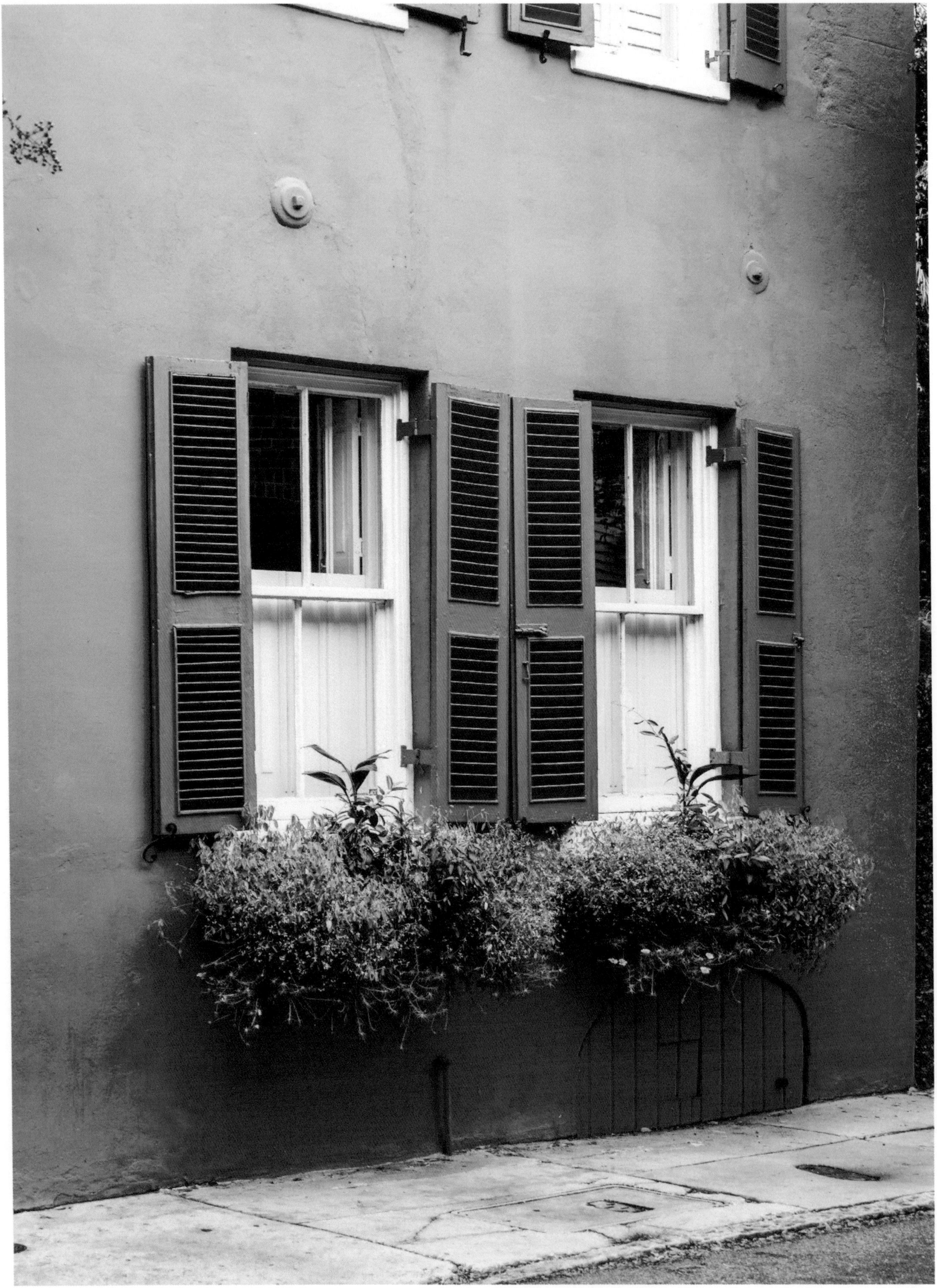

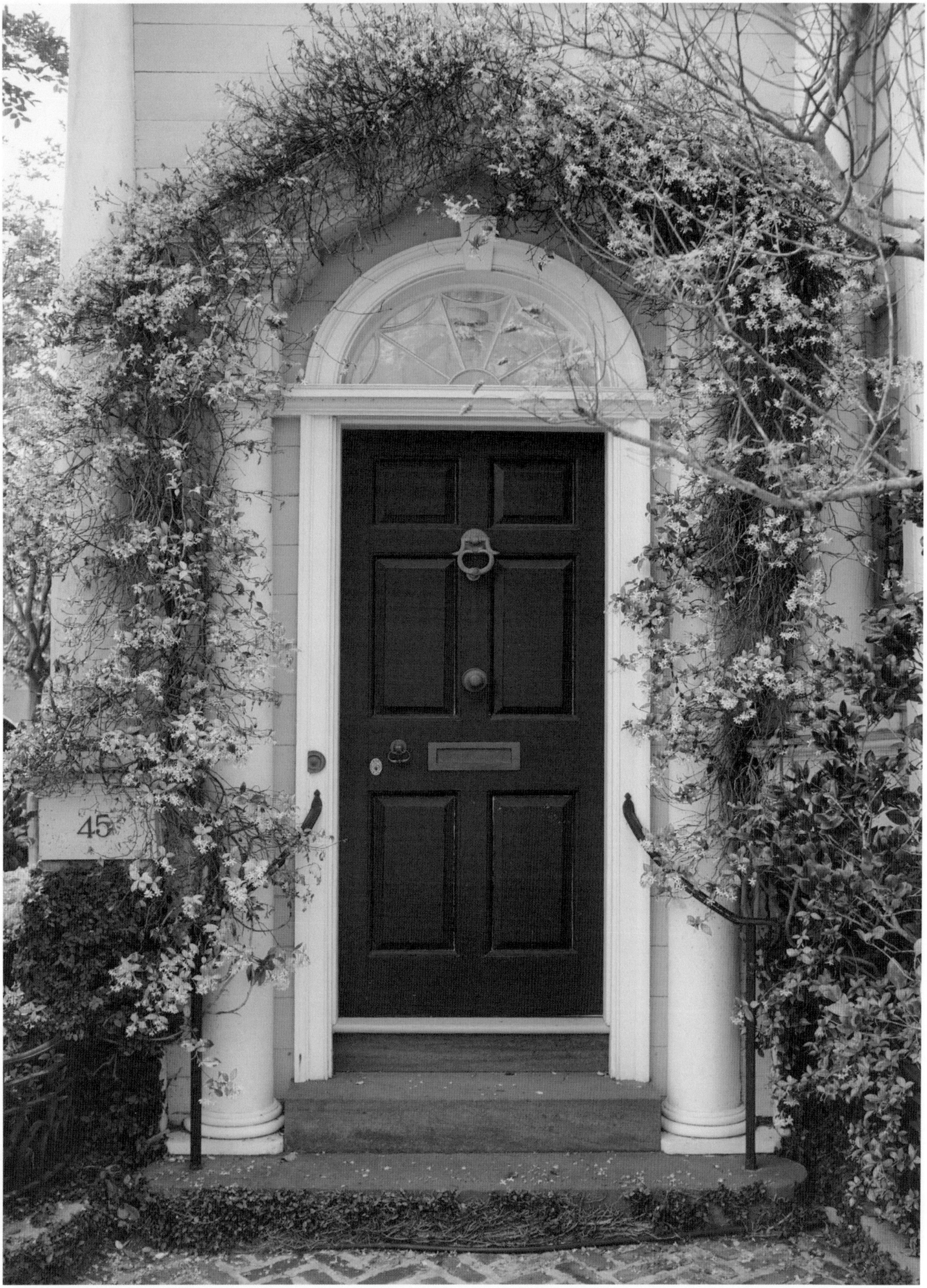
45

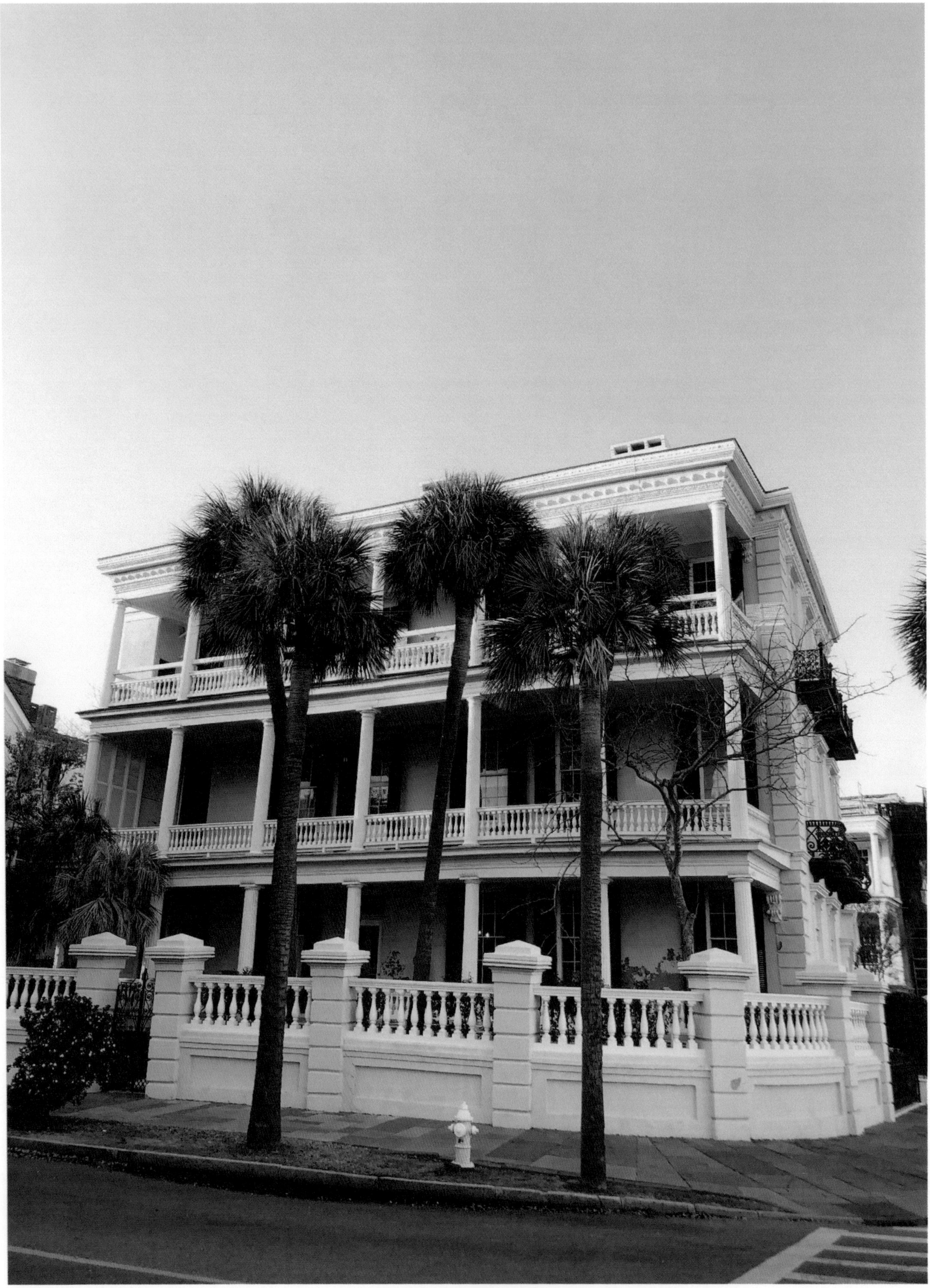

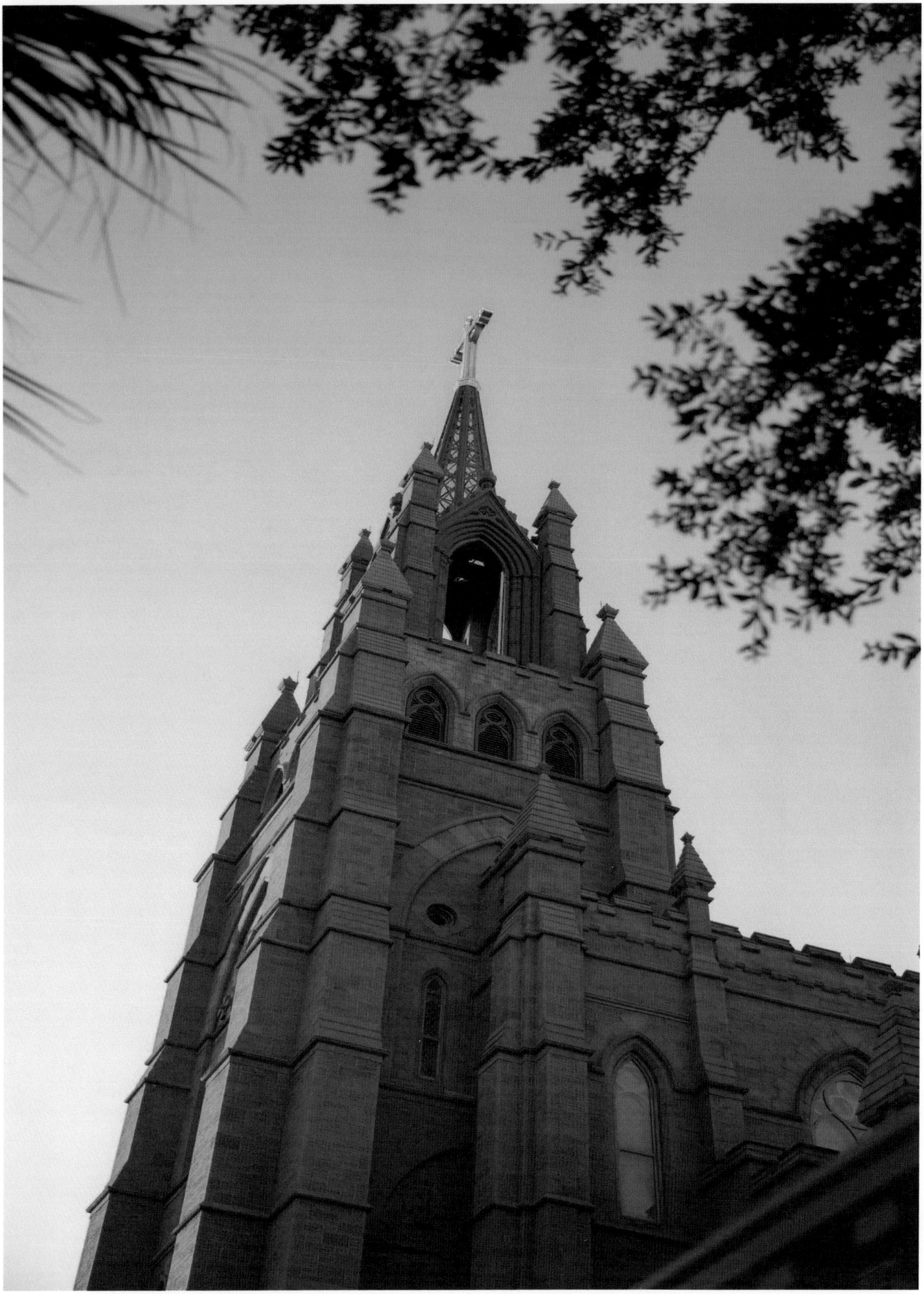

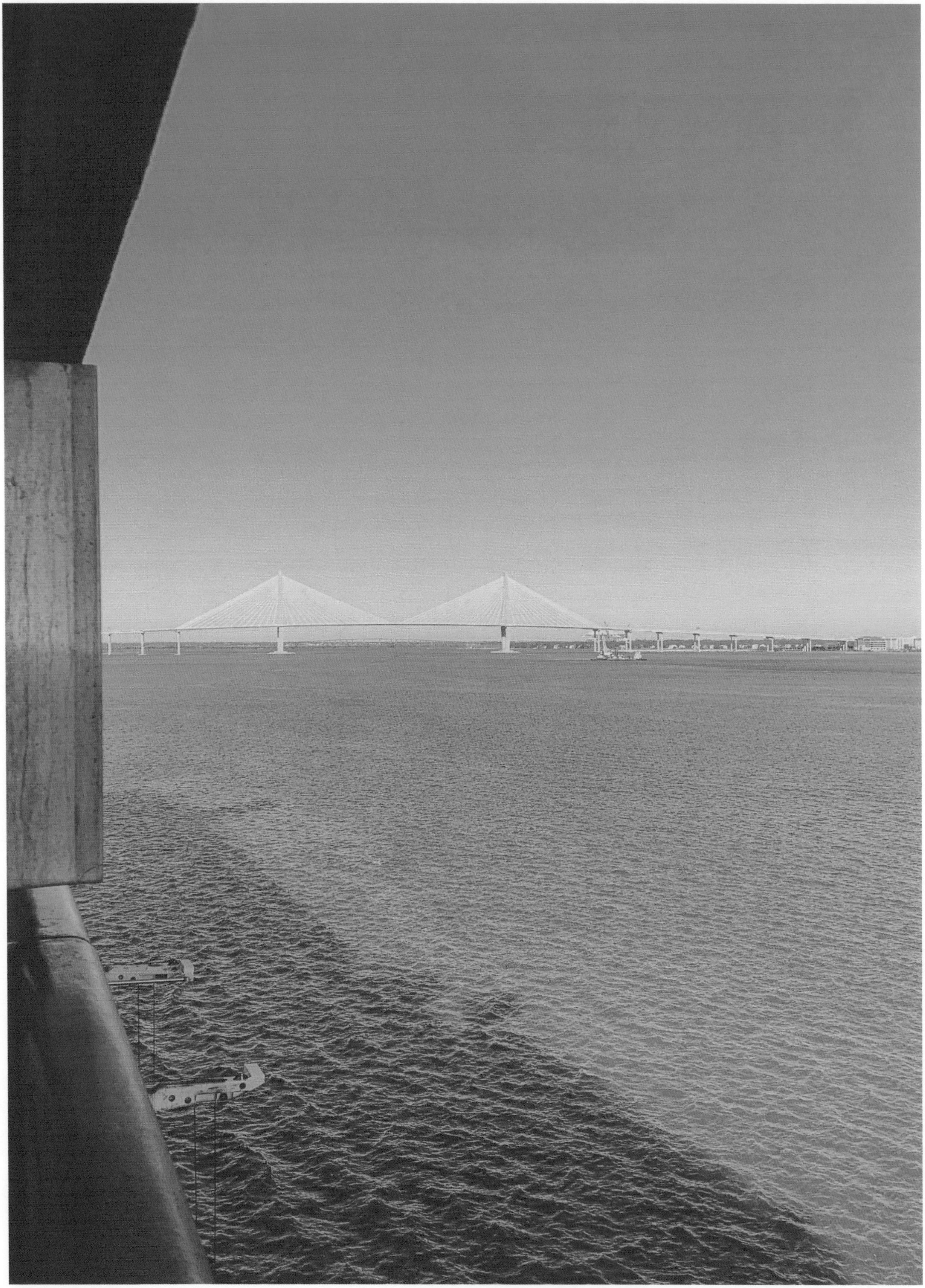

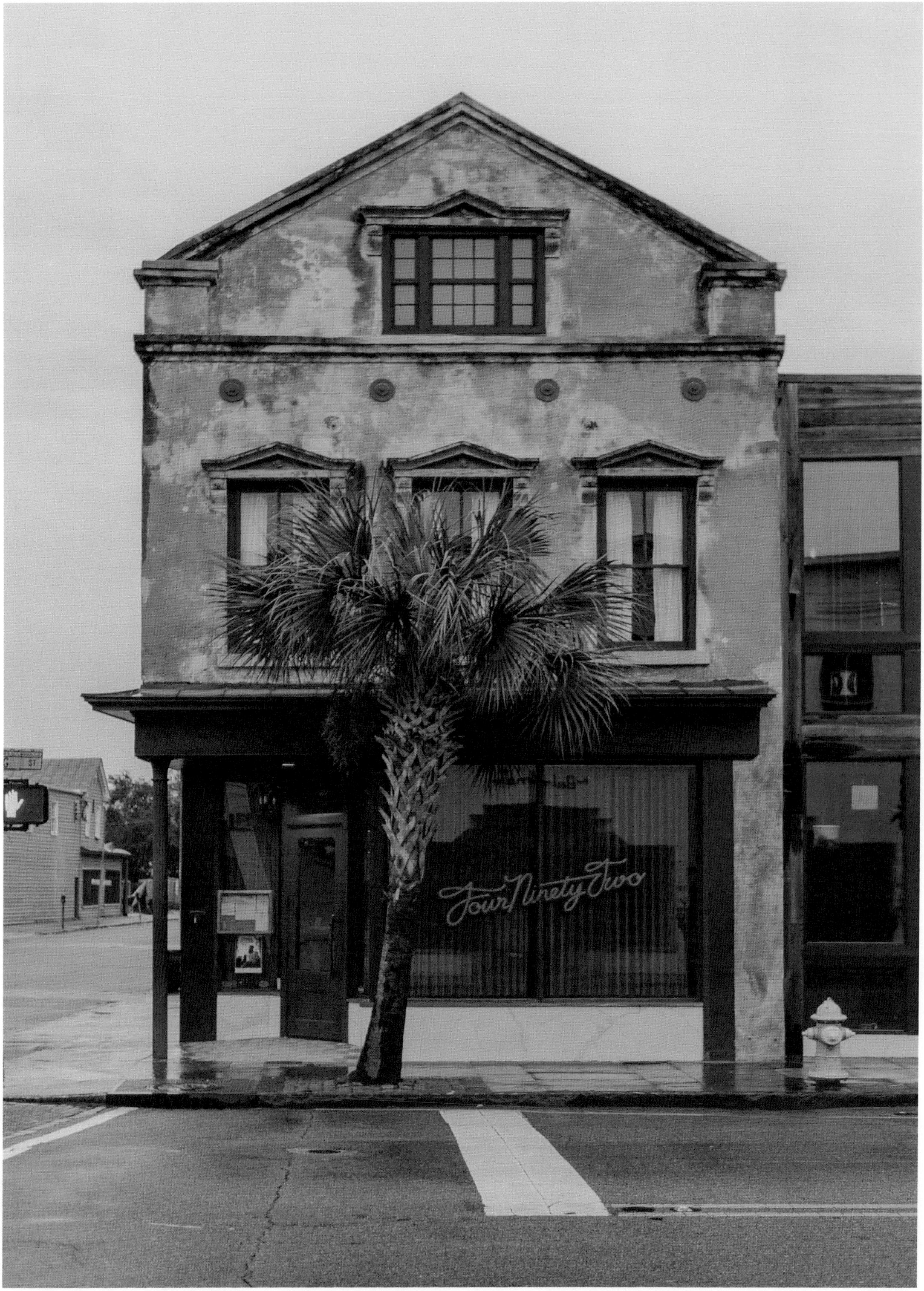
Four Ninety Two

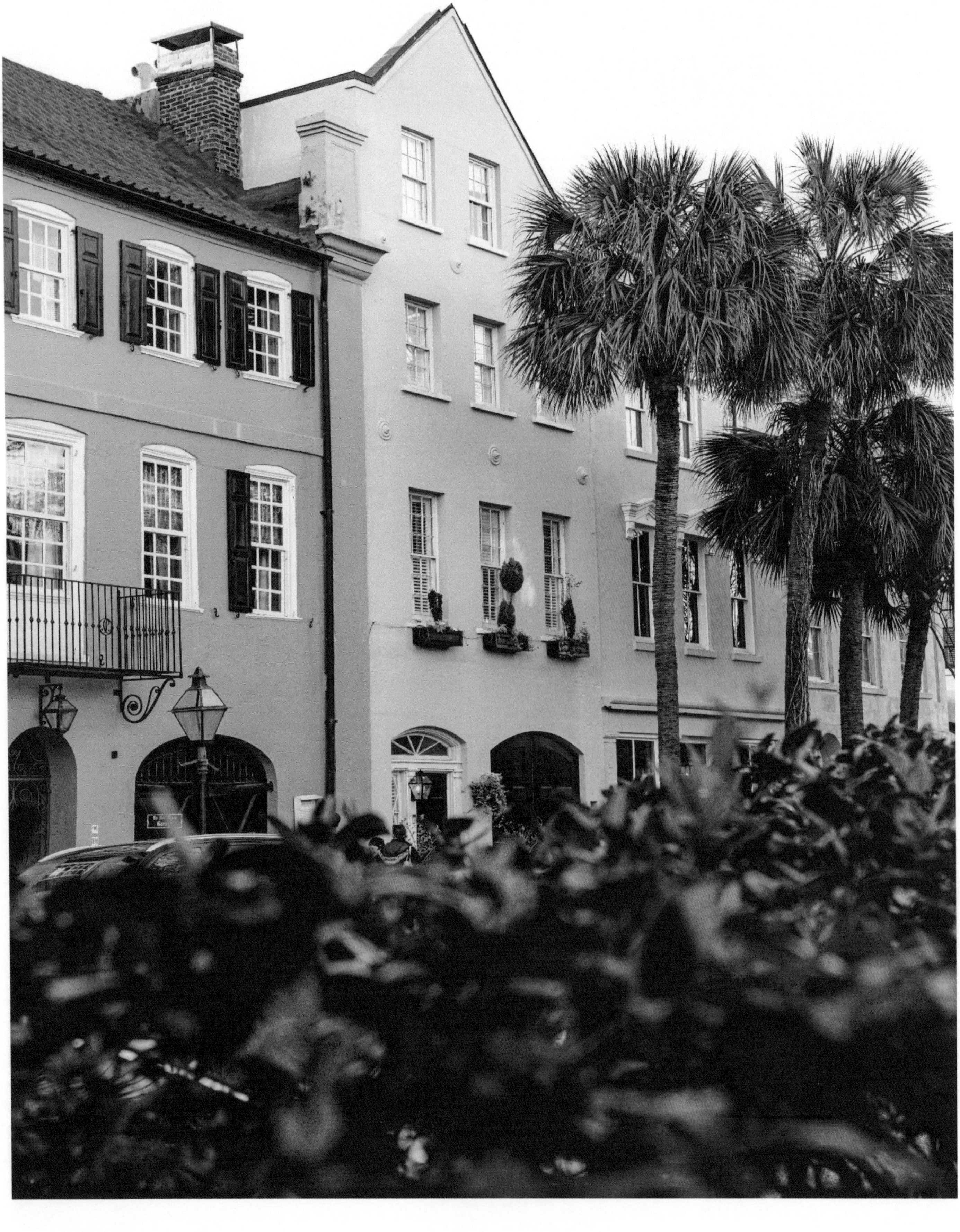

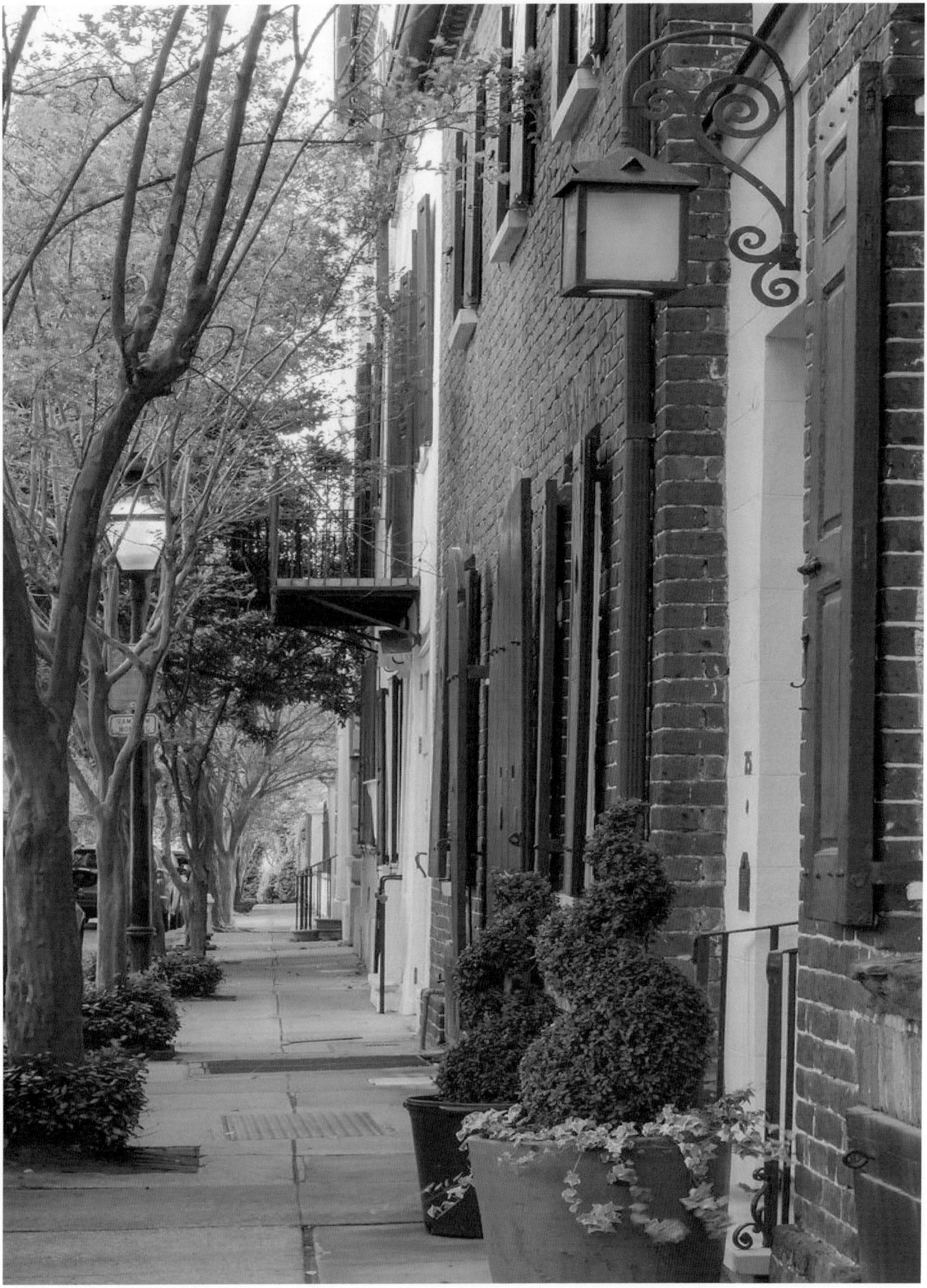

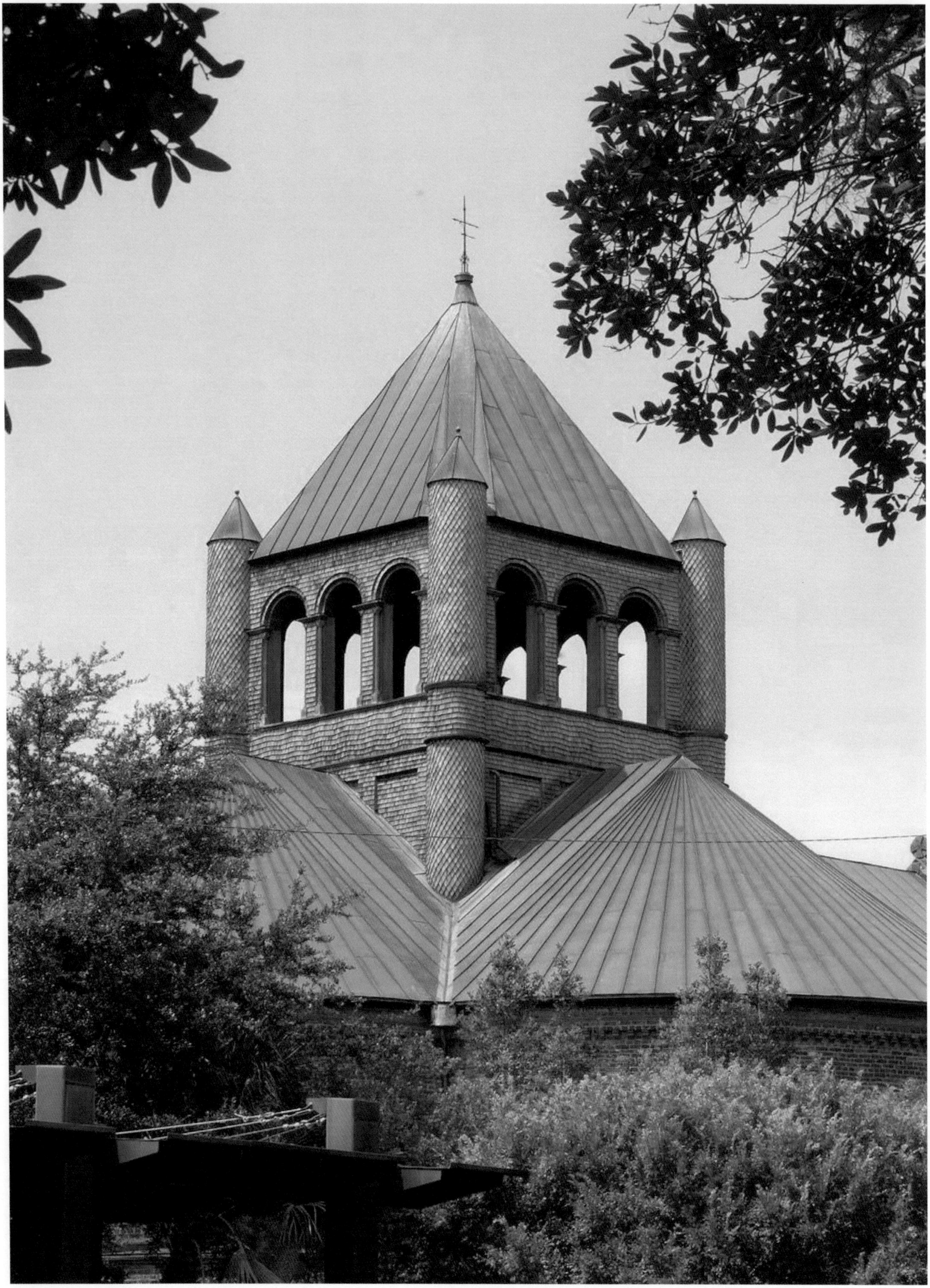

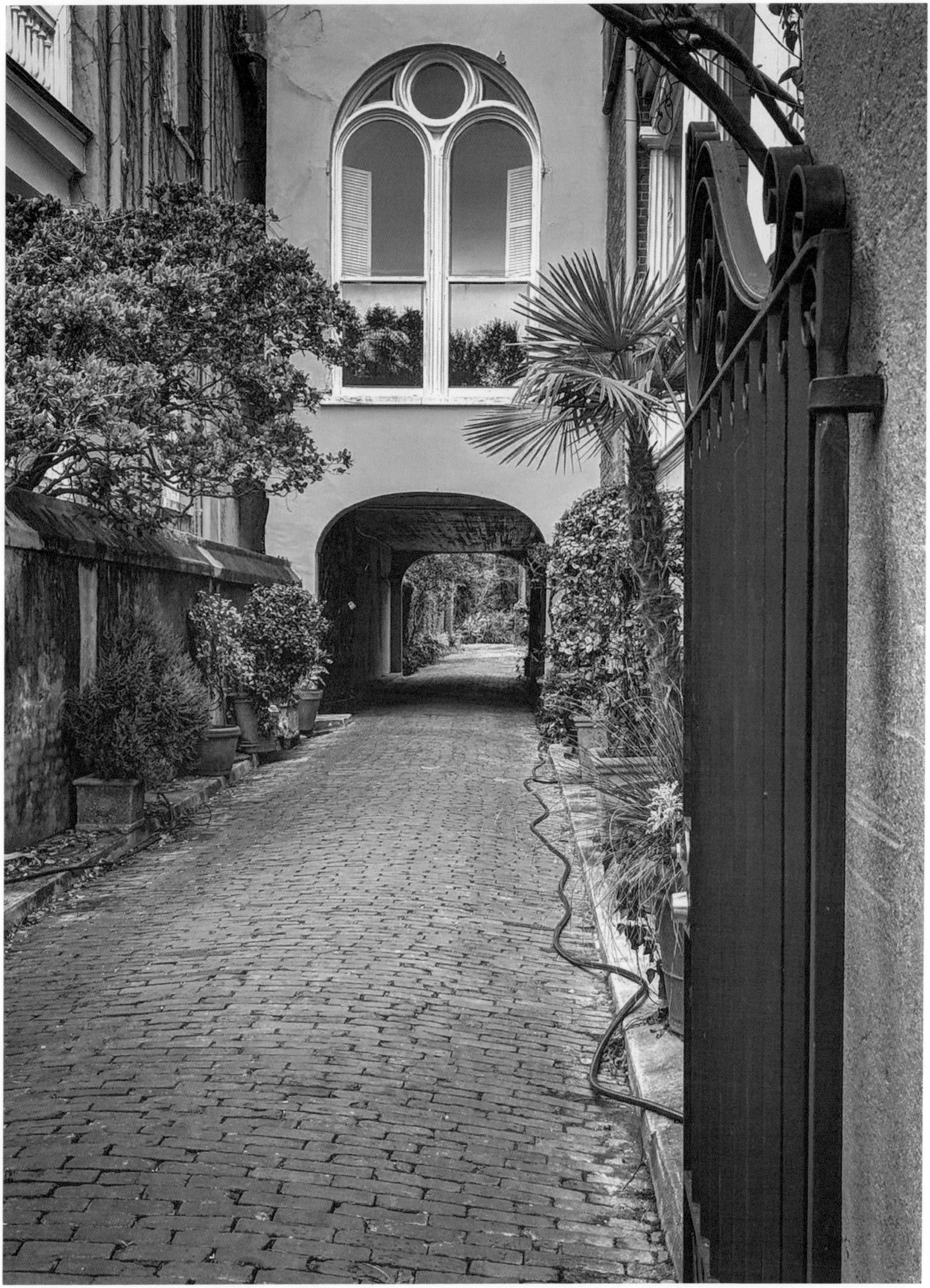

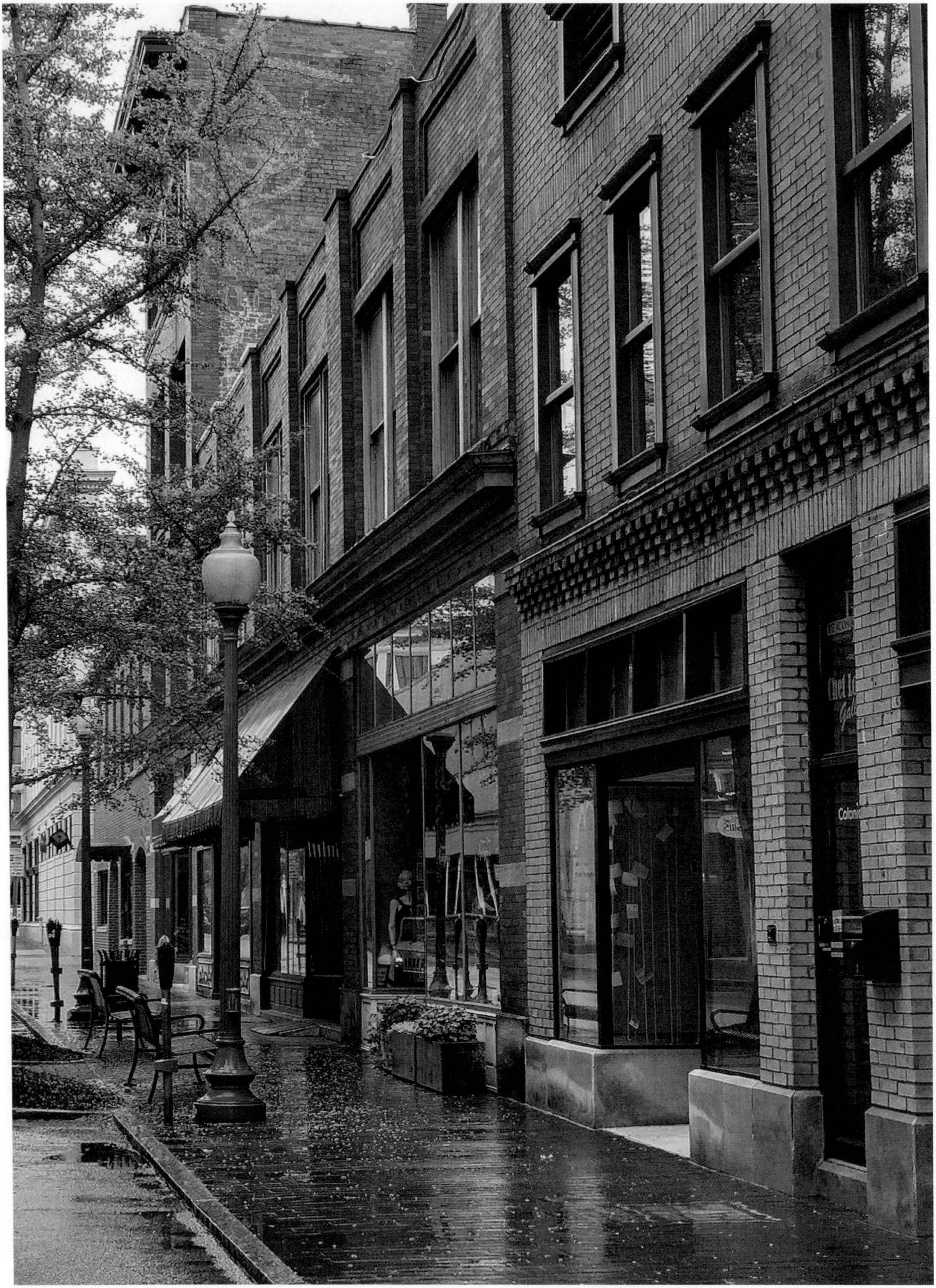

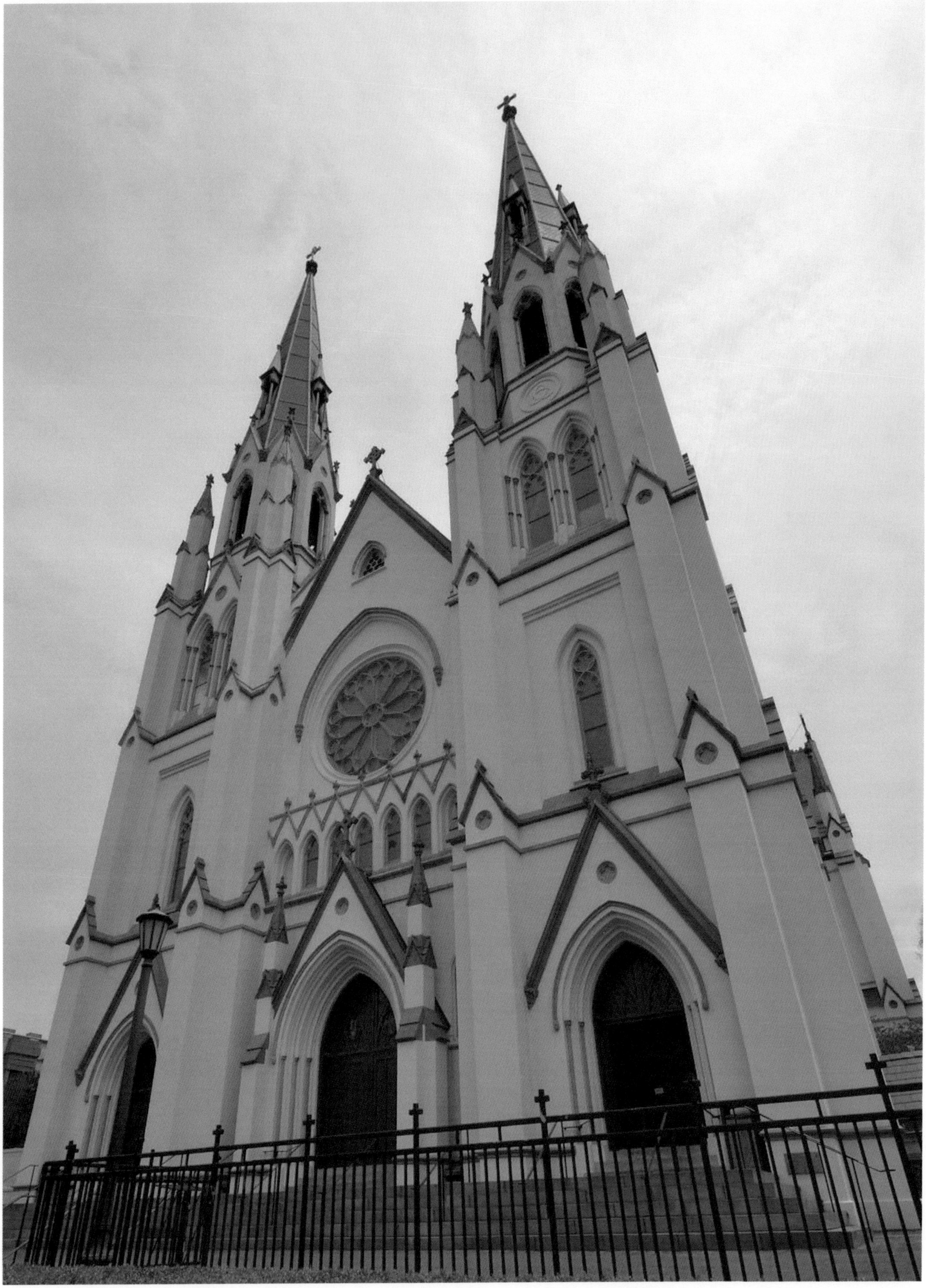

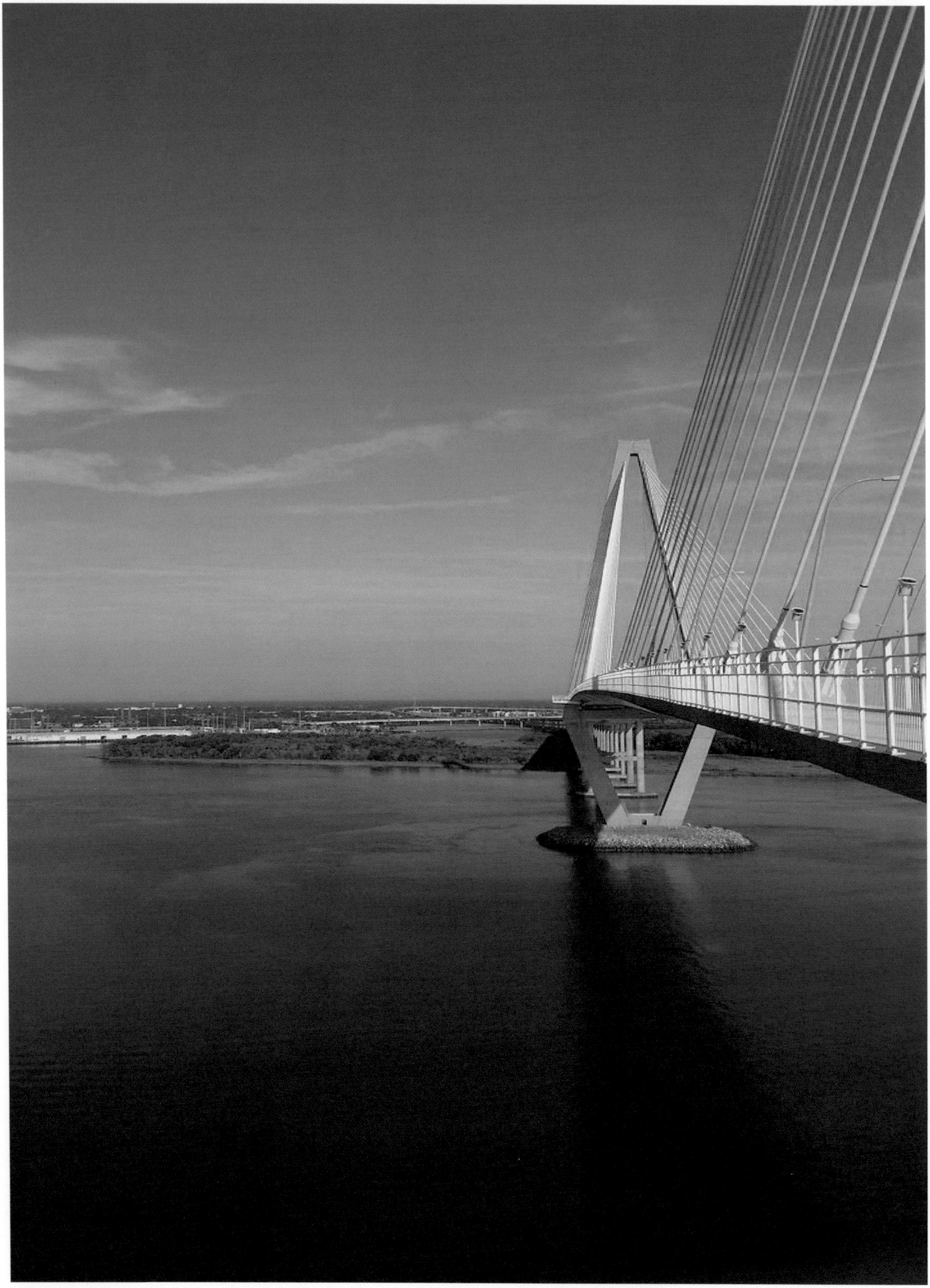

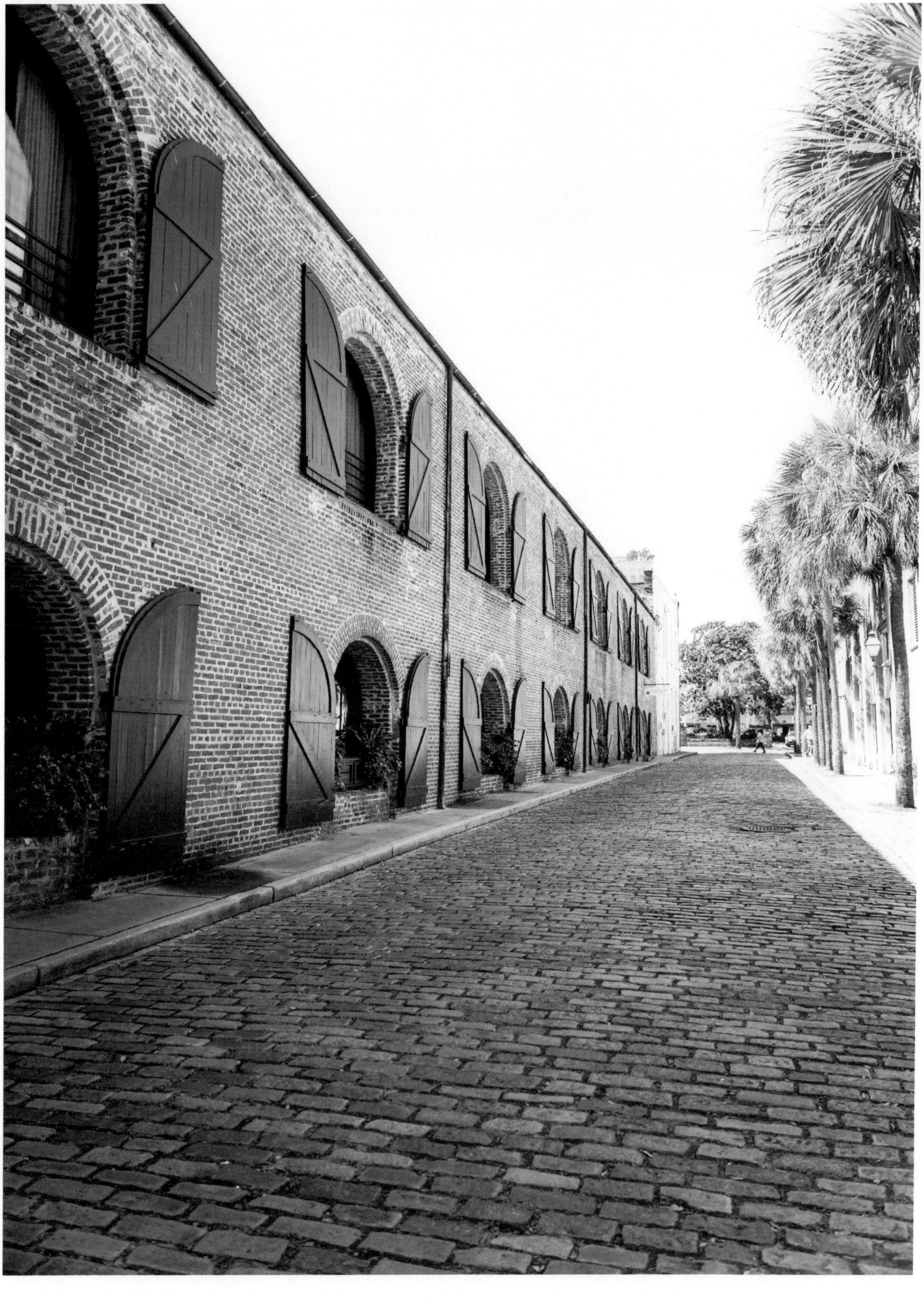

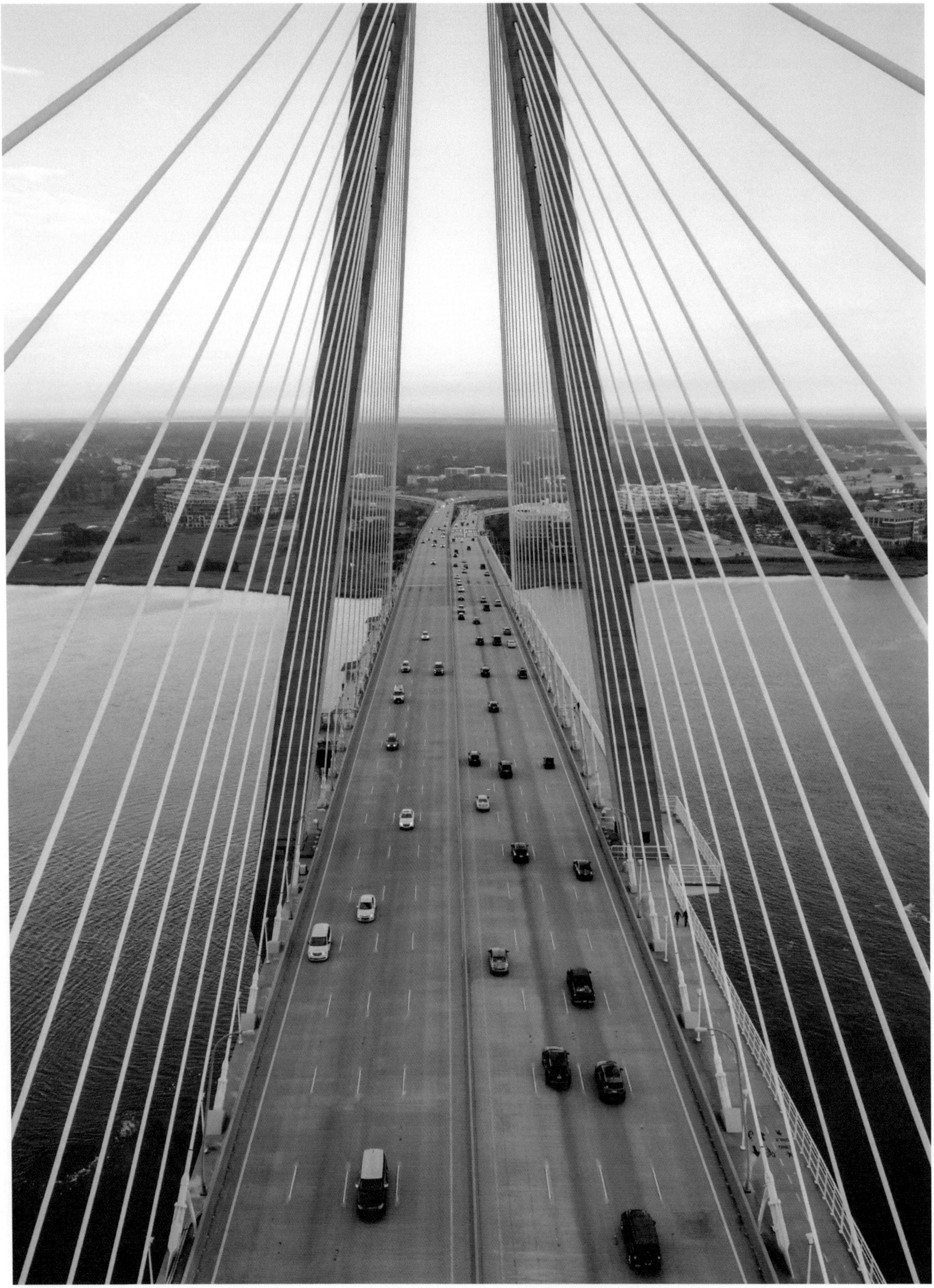

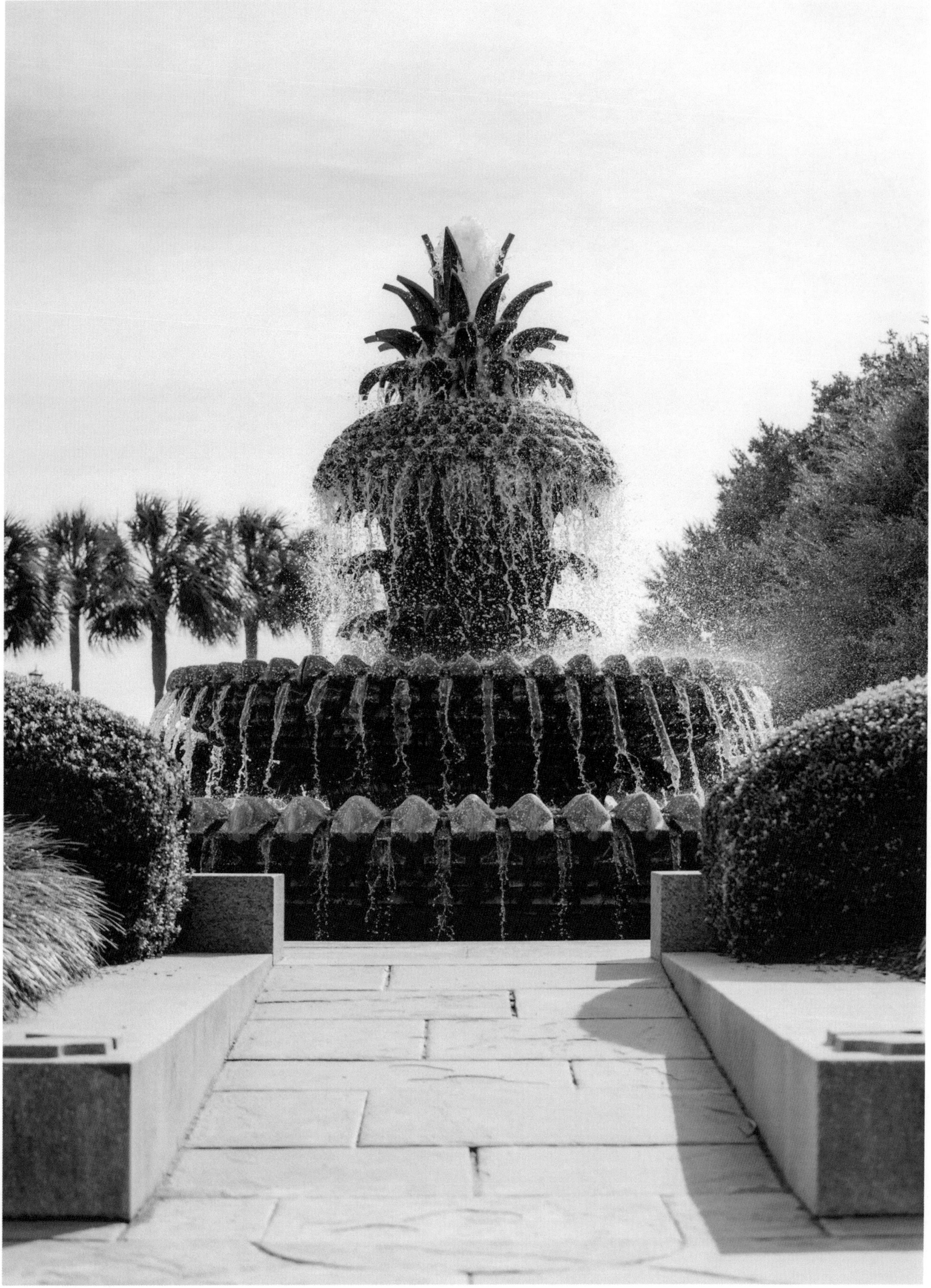

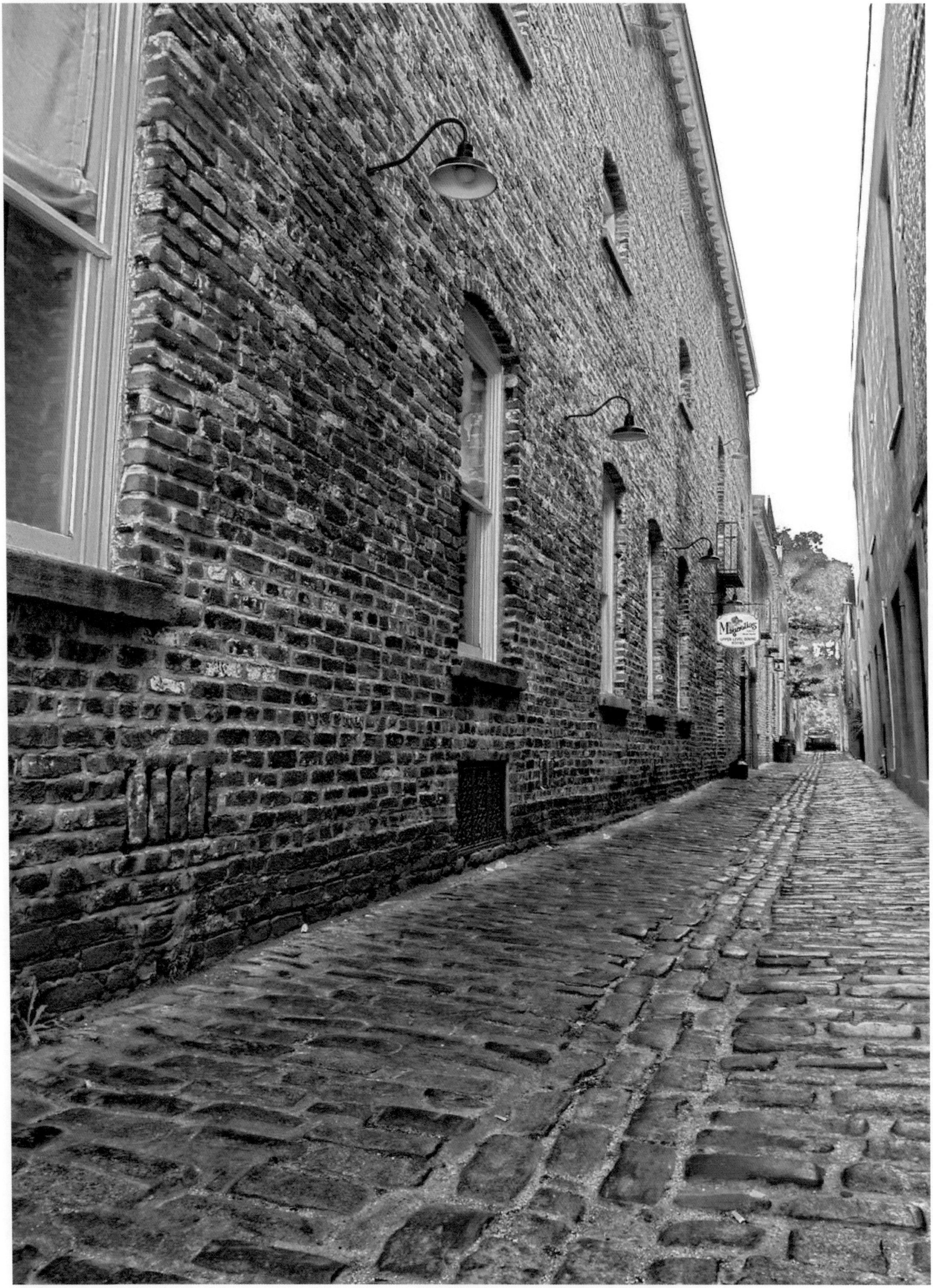

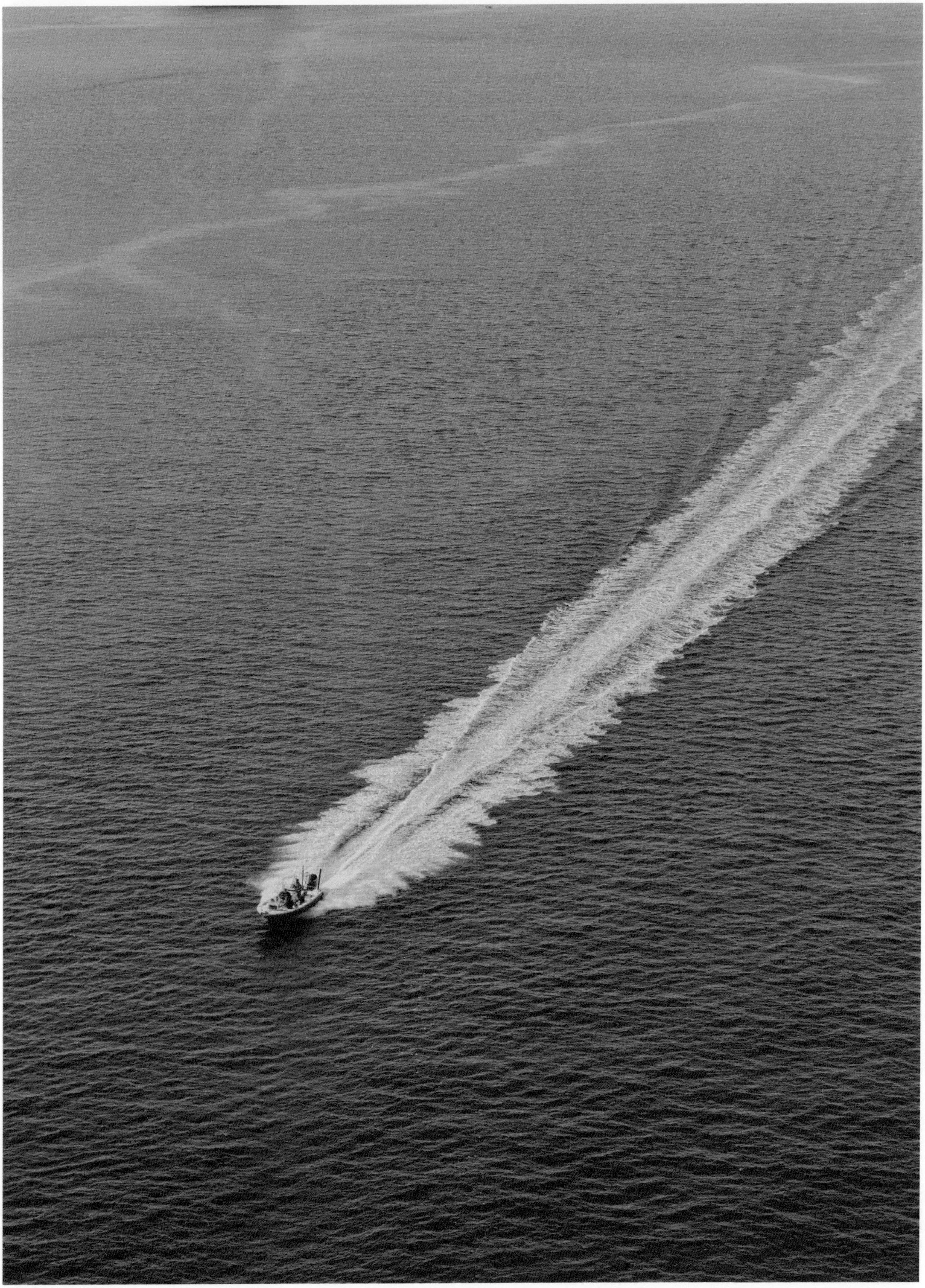

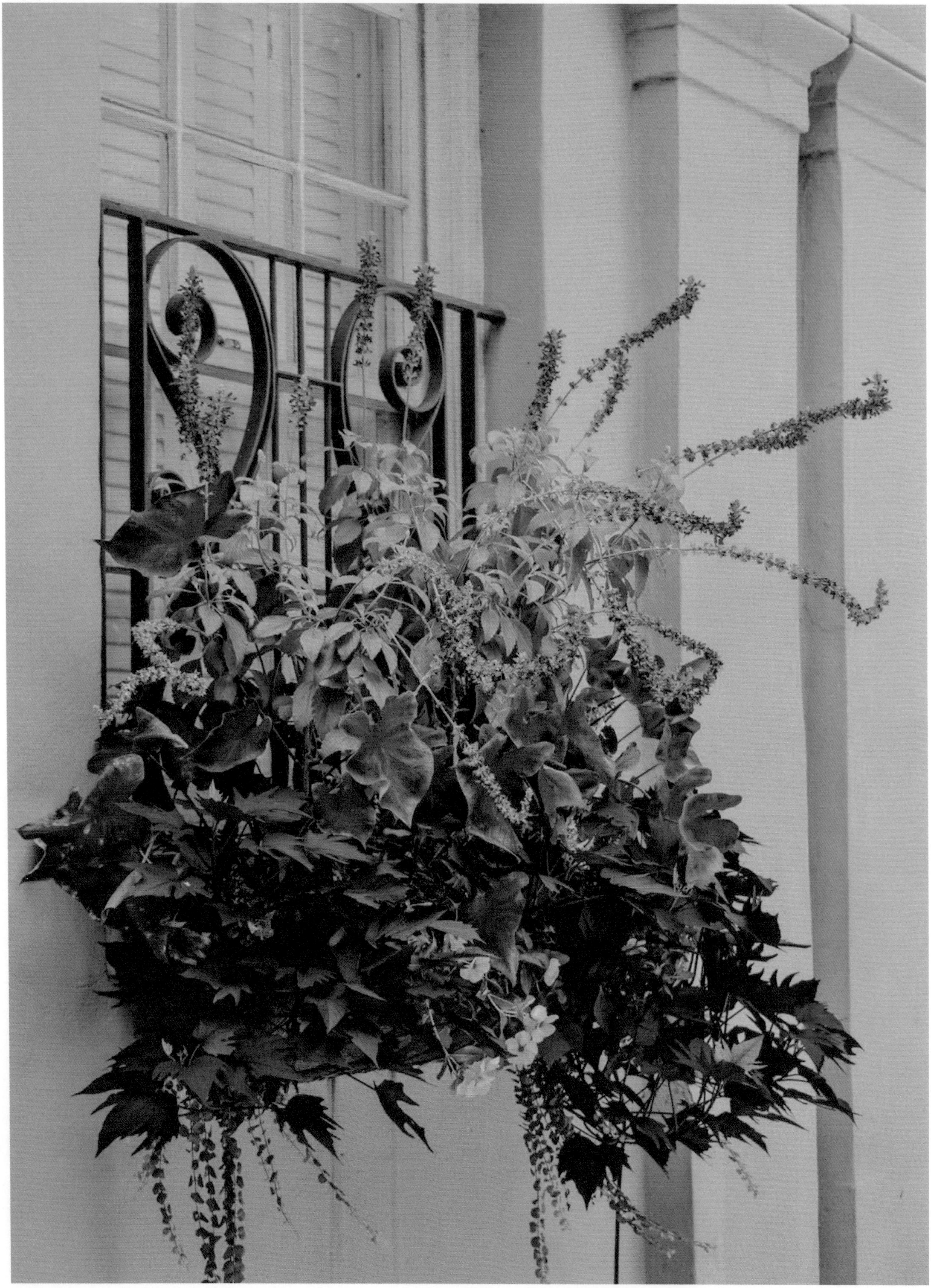

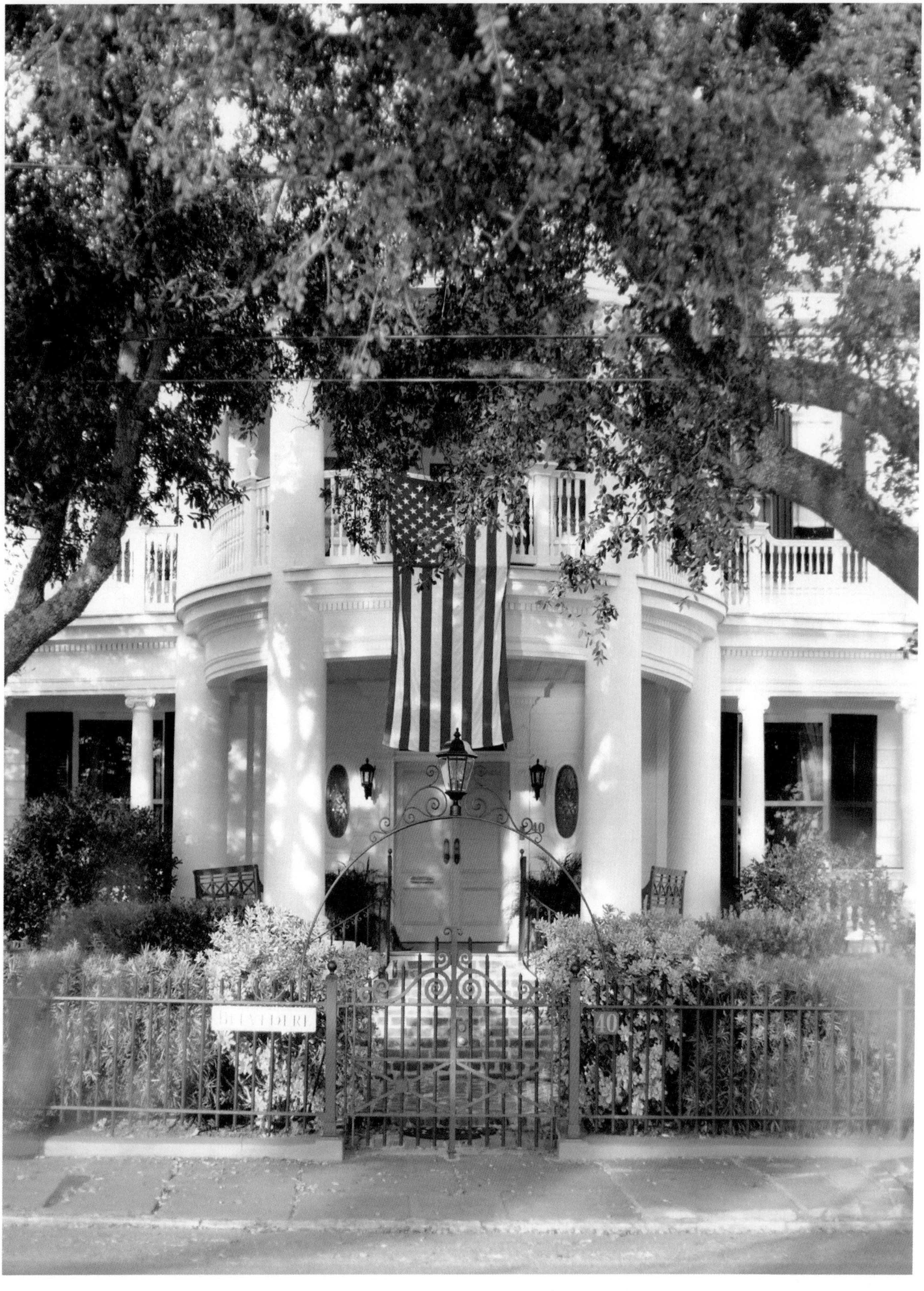
40

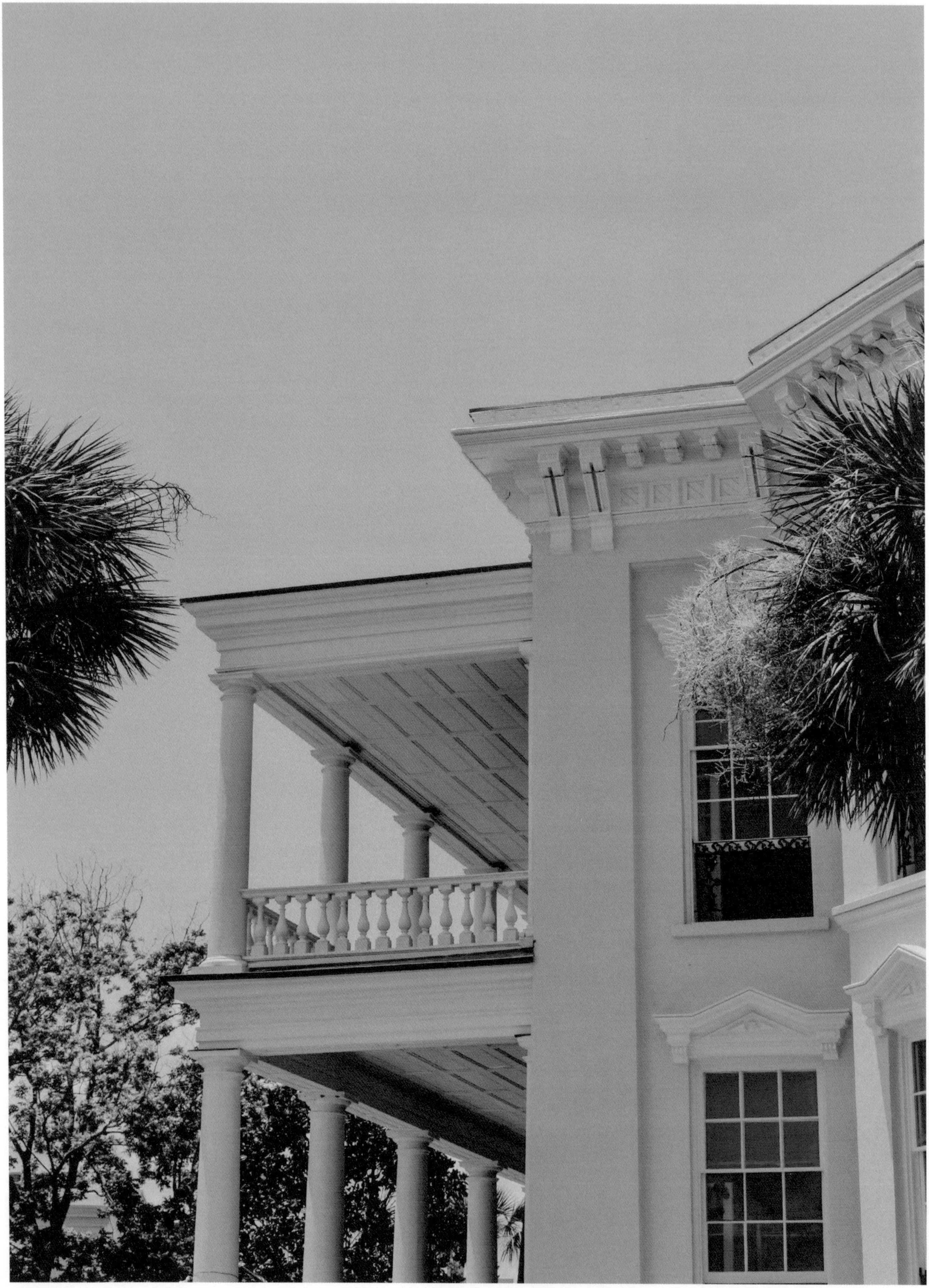

Printed in Great Britain
by Amazon

34704763R00025